Darina Allen

SIMPLY

DELICIOUS
in France & Italy

Gill and Macmillan
and
Radio Telefís Éireann

Published by
Gill & Macmillan Ltd
Goldenbridge
Dublin 8
and
Radio Telefís Éireann
Donnybrook
Dublin 4
© Darina Allen 1992
0 7171 1953 X
Photographs by RTE/Des Gaffney
Food styling by Rory O'Connell
Design by Peter Larrigan
Typeset by Seton Music Graphics Ltd, Bantry, Co. Cork
Colour origination by Colour Studio, Dublin
Printed by ColourBooks Ltd, Dublin

A catalogue record is available for this book
from the British Library.

3   5   4

For Tim, who is still Simply Delicious!

By the same author:
Simply Delicious
Simply Delicious 2
A Simply Delicious Christmas
Simply Delicious Fish
Darina Allen's Simply Delicious Recipes
Simply Delicious Food for Family & Friends
Simply Delicious Versatile Vegetables

Contents

FOREWORD   ix

ACKNOWLEDGMENTS   xi

GLOSSARY   xiii

SOUPS   1
  French Onion Soup   1
  Provençal Soup with Pistou   1
  Italian Fish Soup   3

STARTERS   5
  * Pâté de Campagne with Confiture d'Oignons   5
  * Salade Niçoise   7
  * Salade Tiède with Duck Livers and Marigold Petals   9
  Duck Confit Salad   10
  Black Pudding with Grainy Mustard and Apple Sauce   10
  Carpaccio with Rocket and Parmesan   11
  Crostini di Fegatini   12
  Deep Fried Courgette Flowers   13
  Courgette Flowers Stuffed with Cheese and Tomato   14
  Chargrilled Red and Yellow Peppers   15

EGG AND CHEESE DISHES   16
  Provençal Tomato and Basil Omelette   16
  Provençal Courgette and Basil Omelette   17
  Provençal Terrine with Tomato Sauce   17
  Cheese Soufflé   20
  Gougère   21
  Cheese Galette   23
  Quiche Lorraine   23

FISH   25
  Moules Marinière   25
  Roast Monkfish with Bacon and Sage Butter Sauce   26
  Italian Seafood Salad   27
  Tuna à la Niçoise   28

MEAT 30
 * Boeuf Bourguignon 30
 Fillet of Beef with Pizzaiola Sauce 32
 Fillet of Beef all' Arrabbiata 32
 Fillet of Beef alla Sorrentina 32
 * Pork Roast with Rosemary and Sage 33
 Cassoulet 34
 Rabbit or Chicken with Mustard and Sage Leaves 35
 Chicken Breasts with Parmesan 36
 * Chicken Roast with Whole Cloves of Garlic 37
 * Grilled Duck Breast with Caramelised Apples 38
 * Duck Legs with Onions and Thyme Leaves 39
 * Confit de Canard 40
 Roast Shoulder of Lamb Stuffed with Olives 42

PIZZA 43
 * White Yeast Bread Dough for Pizza 43
 How to Cook Pizzas and Get a Well Browned Bottom! 44
 Pizza Paddle 45
 * Pizza with Caramelised Onions, Blue Cheese and Rosemary 45
 Pizza with Piperonata and Crispy Bacon or Salami 46
 Pizza Face 47
 Pizza Margherita 47
 * Sfinciuni 48
 Calzone 49

PASTA 51
 * Homemade Pasta 51
 Pasta Verde 52
 Pasta with Fresh Herbs 52
 Tomato-flavoured Pasta 53
 * Tagliatelle alla Bolognese 53
 * Ragu 53
 Spaghetti with Pesto 55
 Pasta all' Arrabbiata 56
 Pasta Pizzaiola 56
 Pasta Neapolitana 57
 Spaghetti with Mushrooms, Bacon and Parsley 57
 Spaghetti with Mushrooms, Bacon and Marjoram 57
 Spaghetti with Mushrooms, Bacon and Cream 57
 Spaghetti with Mushrooms, Tuna and Parsley 58
 Marcella Hazan's Pappardelle or Noodles with
  Chicken Liver Sauce 58
 Lasagne Verde 59

Lasagne with Ragu and Piperonata   60
Vegetarian Lasagne   60
How to Make Cappelletti and Tortellini   60
Cappelletti or Tortellini with Butter and Cream   62
Taglierini al Profumo di Limone   63

RISOTTO AND POLENTA   64
 * Risotto alla Parmigiana   65
   Risotto con Ragu   66
   Risotto with Chicken Liver Sauce   66
   Risotto with Dried Mushrooms   66
 * Risotto Primavera   67
 * How to Cook Polenta   68
 * Soft or Wet Polenta   69
 * Chargrilled Polenta   69
 * Chargrilled Polenta with Caramelised Onions and Pesto   69
 * Chargrilled Polenta with Rocket and Olives or Roasted Red
     and Yellow Peppers   69
 * Chargrilled Polenta with Tomato Fondue and Pesto   70
 * Chargrilled Polenta with Gorgonzola, Cashel Blue
     or Goat's Cheese   70

VEGETABLES   71
 * Lentils du Puy   71
   Ratatouille Niçoise   71
   Ratatouille with Olives   72
   Ratatouille with Poached Eggs   73
 * French Beans   73
   Gratin Dauphinois   73
   Rustic Potatoes with Rosemary   74
   Tomato Fondue   75
   Piperonata   76
   Aubergines in Olive Oil   76
   Aubergines with Tomato Fondue and/or Pesto   77
   Aubergines with Tomato and Mozzarella   77
   Julia's Aubergines   77
   Melanzane di Parmigiana   77
   Fennel with Parmesan Cheese   77
   Baked Fennel with Cream and Parmesan   78
   Courgettes (Zucchini) with Marjoram   78
   Green Salad with Goat's Cheese and Sundried Tomatoes   79
   Rocket and Cherry or Sundried Tomato Salad   80
   Sundried Tomatoes   80

DESSERTS   81
  Tarte Tatin   81
* Normandy Pear or Apple Tart   82
  Pine Kernel Tart   84
* How to Line a Flan Ring   84
* Summer Fruit Tart   85
* Plum, Greengage or Apricot Tart   87
  Peach or Nectarine Tart   87
* Confiture de Vieux Garçons   88
* Strawberries in Balsamic Vinegar   89
* Peaches or Nectarines in White Wine   89
  Sugared Peaches with Fresh Lemon Juice   89
* Italian Fruit Salad   90
* Zabaglione   90
  Honey and Lavender Ice-cream   91
* Tira Misu   92
  Nuns' Sighs   93

BREADS   94
  Brioche   94
  Cheese Brioche   95
* Focaccia   96
  Focaccia with Rosemary   96
  Focaccia with Sage   96
  Focaccia with Black Olives   96
* Bruschetta   97
  Bruschetta with Rocket and Black Olive Paste   97
  Bruschetta with Tomatoes and Marjoram or Basil   97
  Bruschetta with Rocket and Roasted Peppers   97
  Bruschetta with Rocket and Shavings of Parmesan   97

The items marked with an asterisk denote recipes which are demonstrated on RTE's *Simply Delicious in France & Italy* television series.

Foreword

I wish everybody could feel the excitement I felt as I travelled through Italy and France tasting and retasting the flavours of two countries which have kept their tradition of regional food wonderfully intact. Dishes which I had enjoyed for years suddenly became even more magical when I ate them on balmy evenings in tiny villages in Tuscany and Provence. The air was perfumed with rosemary and lavender, there were vines and olive trees as far as the eye could see, cicadas chirruped into the night and all of that contributed to the intensity of the experience. Now I want to try to share some of those flavours with you, and I only hope they'll taste every bit as good on a winter's evening in Ireland!

'Peasant' food appeals to me a great deal more than the pretentious dishes we're still being served in so many starred restaurants, so I'm delighted to see that there is now a definite country cooking revival. It is interesting to see how restaurants serving simple, rustic French and Italian food — sensual food, rich with warm, earthy flavours — are packed with customers while the more grandiose places are losing their appeal. That, I think, must say something about the way in which we all crave honest food again.

This simple cooking relies for its impact on superb fresh ingredients. The tradition of buying at the market every day is still strong in France and Italy — and no wonder. People don't decide what they are going to cook until they have made their foray into the bustle of the market place where the open air stalls brimming with bright vegetables, fresh fish, luscious fruit and country cheeses dictate the choice. A ripple of excitement runs through the crowd when the first of a new season's produce arrives — the first spears of asparagus, tiny green peas or porcini. And woe betide the person who is foolish enough to ask for anything that is out of season. The stallholder will heap scorn on them for their stupidity.

In Italy I was enchanted to discover that local produce is so highly prized that people are prepared to pay a premium for it. In the markets it is proudly marked *nostrana* and sought out. Don't they have their priorities right!

Both of these countries are a paradise for food lovers. Cooking traditions have been handed down from generation to generation and food is an immensely important part of each day. Every meal is looked forward to, discussed and, more importantly, shared. In France and even to a greater extent in Italy, the whole country virtually comes to a standstill for two hours at lunchtime so that families can sit down together in a relaxed way. It's an attitude to life that I greatly admire.

In Italy, unlike many other countries, the best food is still to be found in private homes, and interestingly the greatest compliment you can pay a restaurant is to say that the meal was as good as home cooking — *come la cuana di casa*. In both countries the different regions have proudly preserved their specialities. The result is a tremendously rich and varied cuisine. I was interested to discover that in Italy, which is fiercely regional, a speciality of one area may be quite unknown fifty miles down the road — and long may that continue!

From this wealth of possibilities I have tried to choose recipes which are true to the spirit of *Simply Delicious* — things which we can reproduce easily with local ingredients, but which are at the same time very typical of France and Italy. There are some ingredients which may not be so familiar to you, but they are becoming more and more widely available and are essential to the true flavour of the dish, so do seek them out.

Some of my favourite French and Italian recipes are already sprinkled through *Simply Delicious (1)*, *Simply Delicious 2*, *Simply Delicious Fish* and *A Simply Delicious Christmas*, so I don't intend to repeat them here. I have a great many other favourites, however, which sadly lack of space has forced me to exclude. No lovely Osso Bucco, no sensual Provençal Daube and worst of all no flaky, buttery croissants or Gâteau Pithivier. Ah well . . . you'll just have to look out for the next book!

Darina Allen

Shanagarry, Co. Cork.

November 1991

Acknowledgments

I have always loved the sunny flavours of the Mediterranean, so I was delighted when Colette Farmer of RTE suggested we take *Simply Delicious* further afield. She deserves full credit for the idea and for the flair and sheer hard work involved in carrying it through. She was ably assisted once again by her *Simply Delicious* team: Roy Bedell and Kieran Slyne on camera, John Rogers on sound, Liam McDonagh on lights and Kevin Cummins as PA. They were all a tremendous support to me as we battled against sweltering heat in Venice and torrential rains at Châteauneuf-du-Pape. Research for cookery books doesn't normally involve pulling dormobiles out of craters in the road during a storm or rescuing a director stuck fast in the mud!

We were all enormously touched by the welcome and generosity of the people we encountered all the way through France and Italy. A special thank you to Marcella Hazan and her husband Victor; Nataly Rosconi of the Cipriani in Venice, his daughter Francesca and his head chef Renato; Signor Eros of the Restaurant Diana in Bologna; Mimmo Baldi of Il Vescovino in Panzano; Lorenza de' Medici of Badia a Coltibueno; the Avril family at Châteauneuf-du-Pape; Roger Vergé at the Moulin de Mougins and Anne Willan at Château du Fey in Burgundy.

After all that excitement it was back to the Ballymaloe Cookery School kitchen to test and retest recipes. Dervilla O'Flynn, Claire Wenham, Rachel O'Neill and Breda Murphy, ably assisted by Suzanne Walsh and Nina Sisk, were painstaking and heroic. A thank you also to the friends who came over to eat the results and give constructive criticism at the same time.

My two secretaries Rosalie Dunne and Adrienne Morrissey again fed all the recipes into that infernal word processor which still baffles me one year on, and Adrienne gave up much of her spare time to proof with me late into the night. Without her I would still be floundering amid a pile of handwritten pages.

My brother Rory O'Connell once again came to my rescue and, despite a very heavy workload, took charge of the food styling for both the television series and the book. As before, Des Gaffney and his assistant Denis O'Farrell took the photographs with characteristic dedication and flair.

I also want to thank Gill and Macmillan who continue to publish me despite all my grizzling, and a special hug for my long-suffering editor Mary Dowey who has the unenviable task of doing battle with me to keep the book from bursting at the seams.

Once again I want to thank Myrtle and Ivan Allen and my *Simply Delicious* husband Tim for their unwavering support which means so much to me. I've thanked them so many times now that it's difficult to think of a new way to phrase it, but it is sincerely felt nonetheless.

Glossary

Bain marie (or water bath): Can be any deep container, half-filled with hot water, in which delicate foods, e.g. custards or fish mousses, are cooked in their moulds or terrines. The bain marie is put into a low or moderate oven and the food is protected from direct heat by the gentle, steamy atmosphere, without risk of curdling. The term bain marie is also used for a similar container which holds several pans to keep soups, vegetables or stews warm during restaurant service.

Bouquet garni: A small bunch of fresh herbs used to flavour stews, casseroles, stocks or soups, usually consisting of parsley stalks, a sprig of thyme, perhaps a bay leaf and an outside stalk of celery. Remove before serving.

Caramelise: To cook sugar or sugar syrup until it becomes chestnut colour and reaches the caramel stage — 165–175°C (330–350°F).

Confit: Comes from the French word *confire* meaning to preserve. In the case of duck or goose the meat is cooked long and slowly in its own fat and then stored in a cold place submerged in the fat so that the air is excluded.

Deglaze: After meat has been sautéed or roasted, the pan or roasting dish is degreased and then a liquid is poured into the pan to dissolve the coagulated and caramelised pan juices. This is the basis of many sauces and gravies. The liquid could be water, stock or alcohol, e.g. wine or brandy.

Flute: To score the edges of pastry in order to seal and decorate.

Heat diffuser mat: A special gadget made from two layers of perforated metal to put on to a gas jet to diffuse the heat so that a dish can be simmering at the very lowest temperature.

Roux: A basic liaison of butter and flour which is used as a thickening agent. Use equal quantities. Melt the butter, stir in the flour and cook on a low heat for 2 minutes, stirring occasionally. 3 ozs (90 g/$\frac{1}{4}$ cup) of roux will thicken 1 pint (600 ml/$2\frac{1}{2}$ cups) of liquid. The liquid should be boiling as you whisk in the roux, otherwise it won't thicken properly. Roux is tremendously useful to have ready prepared in your kitchen and it will keep in a fridge for several weeks.

Sweat: To cook vegetables in a little fat or oil over a gentle heat in a covered saucepan, until they are almost soft but not coloured.

Terrine: A word used to describe a rough textured pâté or an earthenware dish.

Measurements
All imperial spoon measurements in this book are rounded measurements unless the recipe states otherwise. All American spoon measurements are level.

Temperature Conversion
Approximate fahrenheit/centigrade equivalents are given in the recipes, but for fan or convection ovens it is wise to check the manufacturer's instructions regarding temperature conversion.

Soups

French Onion Soup

Serves 8–10

French onion soup is probably the best known and loved of all French soups. It was a favourite for breakfast in the cafés beside the old markets at Les Halles in Paris and is still a favourite on bistro menus.

> **3 lbs (1.35 kg) onions**
> **2 ozs (55 g/$\frac{1}{2}$ stick) butter**
> **3 pints (1.7 L/$7\frac{1}{2}$ cups) good homemade chicken stock**
>   **(see** *Simply Delicious 1*, **p. 35)** *or* **homemade beef stock**
>   **(see** *Simply Delicious 1*, **p. 46)**
> **salt and freshly ground pepper**
>
> *To finish*
> **8–10 slices of baguette (French bread), $\frac{1}{2}$ inch (1 cm) thick, toasted**
> **4 ozs (110 g/10 American tablesp.) grated Gruyère cheese**

Peel the onions and slice thinly. Melt the butter in a saucepan. Add the onion and cook on a low heat for about 40–60 minutes with the lid off, stirring frequently — the onions should be dark and well caramelised but not burnt. Add the stock, season with salt and freshly ground pepper, bring to the boil and cook for 15 minutes more. Ladle into deep soup bowls, put a piece of toasted baguette covered with grated cheese on top of each one and put under the grill until the cheese melts and turns golden. Serve immediately but beware — it will be very hot. Bon appétit!

Wine suggestion: Côte du Rhône blanc such as Domaine Grangeneuve or a red Côtes du Rhône.

Provençal Soup with Pistou

Serves 10

The mere mention of this soup wafts me back to Provence — one of my favourite places in the whole world. None of the vegetables in this soup is indispensable. They can be replaced by others but the real magic is the pistou.

1

8 ozs (225 g) fresh white haricot beans *or* 6 ozs (170 g/1 cup) dried
    haricot beans, soaked overnight in plenty of cold water
4 pints (2.3L/10 cups) light chicken stock (*Simply Delicious 1*, p. 35)
    or water
3 tablesp. (4 American tablesp.) extra virgin olive oil
salt and freshly ground pepper
2 medium leeks, cut into $\frac{1}{4}$ inch (5 mm) slices
2 small white turnips, cut into $\frac{1}{4}$ inch (5 mm) dice
3 large carrots, cut into $\frac{1}{4}$ inch (5 mm) dice
3 courgettes, cut into $\frac{1}{4}$ inch (5 mm) dice
1 celery stalk, cut into $\frac{1}{4}$ inch (5 mm) dice
2 potatoes peeled and cut into $\frac{1}{4}$ inch (5 mm) dice
4 very ripe tomatoes, peeled and chopped
10 ozs (285 g) small French beans, cut into $\frac{1}{2}$ inch (1 cm) lengths
1 oz (30 g) vermicelli (optional)

Pistou

Pistou is a 'cousin' of the Italian pesto and can be used in a similar way.

5 large cloves garlic
large bunch of fresh basil leaves, 30 large leaves approx.
2 ozs (55 g/$\frac{1}{2}$ cup) freshly grated Parmesan (Parmigiano Reggiano is
    best)
6 tablesp. (8 American tablesp.) extra virgin olive oil

Cover the haricot beans in 4 pints (2.3 L/10 cups) light chicken stock or
water, bring to the boil and cook until just tender, adding some salt
towards the end of the cooking time.

When the haricot beans are almost cooked heat the olive oil in a sauté
pan and toss in all the other ingredients except the French beans and
broken vermicelli if using. Cook for 3–4 minutes, season with salt and
freshly ground pepper, then add to the haricot beans and the cooking
liquid. Cover and simmer for about $\frac{1}{2}$ hour, remove the lid and continue
to simmer for another 15 minutes.

Add the French beans and vermicelli and continue to cook until the
beans are tender — about 8 minutes — adding more water or stock if
necessary.

Meanwhile make the pistou. Peel and crush the garlic well or pound in
a mortar, then add the basil and continue to pound to a paste. Stir in the
grated Parmesan, mix well and then add in the oil drop by drop. (Use a
food processor if you prefer.) Taste the soup, correct the seasoning, pour

into a hot soup tureen, stir the pistou into the soup just before serving and do not boil again. Taste and correct seasoning.

Serve with a bowl of grated Parmesan and a bottle of extra virgin olive oil to drizzle over the soup.

Wine suggestion: Rosé Tavel or any young Provençal rosé, served lightly chilled.

Italian Fish Soup

Serves 10–12

Every port in Italy has its own fish soup and needless to say each one claims that its version is the best — an example of what Italians call their gastronomic *campanilismo*. The technique is usually similar. All seem to use a variety of fish and shellfish simply cooked but some versions have no tomato.

2 lbs (900 g/1 quart) scrubbed mussels, weighed in their shells
   or 1 lb (450 g/1 pint) mussels and 1 lb (450 g/1 pint) clams
3 sprigs parsley
1 sprig thyme
1 sprig fennel
2 teasp. chopped spring onion *or* shallot
8 fl ozs (225 ml/1 cup) dry white wine

2 fl ozs (50 ml/$\frac{1}{4}$ cup) olive oil
4 ozs (110 g/$\frac{3}{4}$ cup) onion, finely chopped
3–4 cloves garlic, finely chopped
1 large red chilli, seeded and finely chopped (optional)
1$\frac{1}{2}$ lbs (675 g) very ripe tomatoes, peeled and chopped
   or 1 x 14 ozs (400 g) tin tomatoes
salt, freshly ground pepper and sugar
2 pints (1.1 L/5 cups) homemade fish stock
   (see *Simply Delicious Fish*, p. 1)

1 lb (450 g) monkfish, cut into $\frac{3}{4}$ inch (2 cm) cubes *or* $\frac{1}{2}$ lb (225 g)
   monkfish and $\frac{1}{2}$ lb (225 g) squid, cut into $\frac{3}{4}$ inch (2 cm) squares
   and scored, with tentacles cut into 1 inch (2 cm) strips
$\frac{1}{4}$ – $\frac{1}{2}$ lb (110–225 g) prawns *or* shrimps in their shells, *or* shelled if
   you prefer

To finish
2 tablesp. (2 American tablesp. + 2 teasp.) freshly chopped parsley
2 teasp. finely chopped fennel leaves

Put the mussels into a non-reactive saucepan with the finely chopped shallot, herbs and dry white wine, cover and steam open on a medium heat (this will take about 5 minutes). Take the mussels out of the liquid just as soon as the shells open, remove and discard the beards and keep the mussels aside, discarding one shell if you like. Strain the liquid and save until later.

Sweat the onion and finely chopped garlic in the olive oil until soft but not coloured (about 5–8 minutes), add the chilli and the chopped tomatoes, season with salt, freshly ground pepper and sugar and cook for 5 minutes. Add the mussel liquor to the tomato with the homemade fish stock, bring to the boil and continue to simmer for 20–30 minutes.*

Just before serving bring back to the boil, add the finely chopped parsley, cubes of monkfish and prawns and simmer for 4–5 minutes or until the fish is just cooked. Put the mussels in their shells and the squid into the soup and add the finely chopped fennel. Taste and correct the seasoning. As soon as the squid turns opaque serve immediately in deep old-fashioned soup bowls, sprinkled with the chopped parsley.

*Can be made ahead to this point

Wine suggestion: Soave, the best known wine of the Veneto, preferably from a single vineyard.

Starters

Pâté de Campagne with Confiture d'Oignons
Country Terrine with Onion Jam — sounds better in French!
Serves 10

Every charcuterie in France proudly sells its own version of Pâté de Campagne. They vary enormously in content and makeup — some are made with rabbit, game and even sweetbreads. A certain proportion of fat is essential, otherwise the terrine will be dry and dull. It is meant to be rough textured so the mixture should not be too finely minced.

> 8 ozs (225 g) fresh chicken livers
> 2 tablesp. (2 American tablesp. + 2 teasp.) brandy
> $\frac{1}{2}$ teasp. ground white pepper (yes, put it all in!)
> 8 ozs (225 g) very thinly sliced, rindless streaky rashers (you may
>   need more if they are not very thinly sliced) *or* better still,
>   barding fat*
> $\frac{1}{2}$ oz (15 g /$\frac{1}{8}$ stick) butter
> 1 medium onion finely chopped
> 1 lb (450 g) streaky pork, minced
> 8 ozs (225 g) stewing veal, minced (substitute chicken if you can't
>   get veal)
> 2 cloves garlic, finely chopped
> $\frac{1}{4}$ teasp. ground allspice (pimento)
> a good pinch of ground cloves
> $\frac{1}{2}$–1 teasp. freshly chopped annual marjoram (optional)
> 2 small eggs, beaten
> salt, freshly ground pepper and nutmeg
> 2 ozs (55 g) shelled pistachios
> 6–8 oz (170–225 g) piece of cooked ham, cut in thick strips
> bay leaf
> sprig of thyme
>
> luting paste (see below) *or* tinfoil
>
> 3 pint (1.7 L/7$\frac{1}{2}$ cup) capacity terrine *or* casserole with tight fitting
>   lid

*Sean Loughnane, 56 Dominick Street, Galway will supply barding fat and caul fat to order. Both can be frozen.

Wash the chicken livers, separate the lobes and remove any trace of green. Marinade in the brandy and $\frac{1}{2}$ teasp. of ground white pepper for 2 hours. Line a terrine or casserole with very thinly sliced bacon or barding fat, keeping a few slices for the top.

Sweat the onion gently in the butter until soft but not coloured. Mix the onion with the pork, veal, garlic, allspice, ground cloves, chopped marjoram, beaten eggs and the brandy from the chicken livers. Season with salt, freshly ground pepper and lots of grated nutmeg. Mix very thoroughly. Fry a little piece and taste for seasoning — it should taste quite spicy and highly seasoned. Add the pistachios and beat until the mixture holds together.

Spread a third of the *farce* in the lined terrine, add a layer of half the ham strips interspersed with half the chicken livers, then cover with another third of the pork mixture. Add the remaining ham and livers and cover with the last third. Lay the reserved barding fat or bacon slices on top, trimming the edges if necessary. Set the bay leaf and sprig of thyme on top of the bacon or barding fat and cover with the lid. Seal the lid with luting paste (see below) or else use a sheet of tinfoil under the lid.

Cook in a bain-marie in a preheated oven, 180°C/350°F/regulo 4, for $1\frac{1}{4}$–$1\frac{1}{2}$ hours or until a skewer inserted for $\frac{1}{2}$ minute into the mixture is hot to the touch when taken out. If you are still in doubt remove the lid and check: the pâté should also have shrunk in from the sides of the terrine and the juices should be clear.

Cool until tepid, remove the luting paste or tinfoil and lid and press the terrine with a board and a 2 lb (900 g) weight until cold. This helps to compact the layers so that it will cut more easily. Keep for 2–3 days before serving to allow the terrine to mature. It can be frozen for up to 2 months.

To serve: Unmould the terrine, cut into thick slices as needed and serve with Confiture d'Oignons (see p. 7), a good green salad and a glass of red wine. Gherkins and olives are often served as an accompaniment in France.

Wine suggestion: A full bodied red wine. If you want a real treat with an Irish connection, have a Château Lynch-Bages from Bordeaux — but Gigondas or Le Petit Vin d'Avril from the Rhône would be less expensive and excellent also.

Luting paste

> **8 ozs (225 g/1$\frac{1}{2}$ cups) flour**
> **5–6 fl ozs (150–175 ml/generous $\frac{1}{2}$–$\frac{3}{4}$ cup) approx. water**

Mix the flour and water into a dough firm enough to handle, roll into a rope and use to seal the lid on to the casserole to prevent the steam from escaping during cooking.

Confiture d'Oignons

Makes $\frac{3}{4}$ pint (450 ml)

This superb recipe has become very popular in recent years and I always have some made up. It is wonderful warm also, particularly with pan-grilled monkfish or even a lamb chop.

> $1\frac{1}{2}$ lbs (675 g) onions
> 4 ozs (110 g/1 stick) butter
> $1\frac{1}{2}$ teasp. salt
> $\frac{1}{2}$ teasp. pepper, freshly ground
> $5\frac{1}{2}$ ozs (155 g/$\frac{3}{4}$ cup) castor sugar
> 7 tablesp. (9 American tablesp.) sherry vinegar
> 2 tablesp. (2 American tablesp. + 2 teasp.) cassis
> scant $\frac{1}{2}$ pint (250 ml/$1\frac{1}{4}$ cups) full bodied red wine

Peel and slice the onions thinly. Heat the butter in the saucepan until it becomes a deep nut brown (*beurre noisette*) — this will give the onions a delicious flavour but be careful not to let it burn. Toss in the onions and sugar, add the salt and freshly ground pepper and stir well.

Cover the saucepan and cook for 30 minutes over a gentle heat, keeping an eye on the onions and stirring from time to time with a wooden spatula. Add the sherry vinegar, red wine and cassis. Cook for a further 30 minutes uncovered, stirring regularly (but don't let them reduce too much). This onion jam must cook very gently. When it is cold, skim off any butter which rises to the top and discard.

Confiture d'Oignons will keep for months and is especially delicious with pâtés and terrines of meat, game and poultry.

*Salade Niçoise

Serves 8 approx.

In Provence there are many versions of this colourful salad which makes a wonderful summer lunch. Some include crisp red and green pepper and others omit the potato for a less substantial salad.

French dressing
2 fl ozs (50 ml/scant $\frac{1}{4}$ cup) wine vinegar
6 fl ozs (175 ml/$\frac{3}{4}$ cup) extra virgin olive oil
2 large cloves garlic, mashed
$\frac{1}{2}$ teasp. Dijon mustard
good pinch of salt and freshly ground pepper
1 tablesp. (1 American tablesp. + 1 teasp.) parsley,
    chopped
1 tablesp. (1 American tablesp. + 1 teasp.) basil
    or annual marjoram

Salad
8 medium sized new potatoes (e.g. Pink Fir Apple),
    cooked but still warm
3–4 ripe tomatoes, peeled and quartered
4 ozs (110 g) cooked French beans, topped and tailed and cut
    into 2-inch (5 cm) lengths approx., blanched and refreshed
salt, freshly ground pepper and sugar
1 dessertsp. (2 American teasp.) chives
1 dessertsp. (2 American teasp.) parsley, chopped
1 dessertsp. (2 American teasp.) annual marjoram *or* thyme
1 crisp lettuce
3 hardboiled eggs, shelled and quartered
12 black olives
1 teasp. capers (optional), salted if possible
1 tin anchovies, salted if possible *and/or* 1 tin tuna fish
8 tiny spring onions

Mix all the ingredients for the dressing together — it must be very well seasoned, otherwise the salad will be bland. Slice the new potatoes into $\frac{1}{4}$ inch (5 mm) thick slices and toss in some dressing while still warm. Season with salt and freshly ground pepper. Toss the tomatoes and beans in some more dressing, season with salt, pepper and sugar and sprinkle with some chopped herbs.

Line a shallow bowl with lettuce leaves. Arrange the rest of the ingredients appetisingly on top of the potatoes, finishing off with olives, capers and chunks of tuna and/or the anchovies. Drizzle some more dressing over the top. Scatter with the remainder of the herbs and the spring onions and serve.

Wine suggestion: Chilled Côtes du Luberon or Côtes de Provence or a Provençal rosé.

*Salade Tiède with Duck Livers and Marigold Petals

Serves 4

Salades tièdes or warm salads are a legacy of the Nouvelle Cuisine movement which began in the early 1970s in France. This sort of salad was, and indeed still is, very typical and makes a light and delicious starter. A few cubes of Rustic Potatoes with Rosemary (see p. 74) would also be delicious on this salad.

Salad
a selection of lettuce and salad leaves e.g. butterhead, iceberg, oakleaf, lollo rosso, curly endive and misticana
1 dessert apple, peeled and diced
$\frac{1}{2}$ oz (15 g/$\frac{1}{8}$ stick) approx. butter
4–6 fresh duck livers *or* if unavailable, chicken livers
salt and freshly ground pepper
$\frac{1}{2}$ oz (15 g/$\frac{1}{8}$ stick) butter

Dressing
3 tablesp. (4 American tablesp.) extra virgin olive oil
1 tablesp. (1 American tablesp. + 1 teasp.) red wine vinegar
a little Dijon mustard
salt and freshly ground pepper

Garnish
1 tablesp. (1 American tablesp. + 1 teasp.) chopped chives
chive flowers
marigold petals

Wash and dry the salad leaves and tear into bite-sized pieces. Whisk together the ingredients for the dressing. Fry the apple dice in a little butter until just soft and almost golden and taste — they may need a pinch of sugar. Keep warm. Wash and dry the livers and divide each one into 2 pieces.

Just before serving, melt the second quantity of butter in a sauté pan, season the livers with salt and freshly ground pepper and cook over a gentle heat. While the livers are cooking, toss the salad leaves in just enough dressing to make the leaves glisten. Divide the salad between 4 large plates, sprinkle with the apple dice, divide the hot livers evenly between each salad (they are very good slightly pink in the centre but only if you like them that way). Sprinkle with chopped chives, chive flowers and marigold petals and serve immediately.

Note: You can do lots of variations on this starter. You could also cook the fillet pieces from the duck breasts (see p. 38) quickly on a pan and slice them on to this salad.

Wine suggestion: A light red, e.g. Fleurie from Beaujolais or a full-bodied Crozes-Hermitage from the Rhône Valley.

Duck Confit Salad

Serves 4

> **ingredients as above but substitute 2 preserved duck legs for chicken livers (see Duck Confit recipe, p. 40)**

Remove the duck legs from the fat (it may be necessary to melt some of it). Preheat the oven to 180°C/350°F/regulo 4. Roast the duck for 15–20 minutes and then cook for 4–5 minutes on a hot grill pan to crisp the skin. Strip the crispy duck from the bones and divide between the four plates of salad. Sprinkle with chopped chives, chive flowers and marigold petals as described above. Serve immediately.

Wine suggestion: A medium red such as St Emilion or a Beaujolais, e.g. Juliénas.

Black Pudding with Grainy Mustard and Apple Sauce

Serves 12 for canapés, 4–6 as a starter

The French serve their black pudding for lunch or dinner accompanied by mounds of fluffy Golden Delicious apples and potato purée. It is also very good served on buttery croûtons as a canapé or starter.

> **12 slices French bread *or* 12 x 2 inch (5 cm) rounds white bread**
> **butter *or* olive oil**
> **12 slices best quality black pudding approx. $\frac{1}{2}$ inch (1 cm) thick**
> **Moutarde de Meaux *or* Lakeshore whole grain mustard with honey**
> **apple sauce made with Golden Delicious apples (see *Simply Delicious 2*, p. 43)**
>
> *Garnish*
> **flat parsley *or* watercress**

Brush both sides of the bread with butter or olive oil. Cook on a baking sheet in a moderate oven, 180°C/350°F/regulo 4, until golden on both sides (20 minutes approx.). Drain on kitchen paper and keep warm.

Melt a very little butter in a frying pan and fry the black pudding on both sides on a medium heat. Meanwhile spread a little grainy mustard on each warm croûton. Remove the skin from the black pudding. Put a piece of hot pudding on to each croûton and top with a blob of apple sauce. Serve 2 or 3 croûtons per person on a hot plate garnished with flat parsley or watercress.

Wine suggestion: Cahors or Madiran from southwest France.

Carpaccio with Rocket and Parmesan

Serves 12

Carpaccio is the ultimate recipe to make a little beef go a very long way. This sophisticated dish was invented in Harry's Bar in Venice and named for Carpaccio, the great 15th-century Venetian painter. There are many variations and this one is inspired by a version served at the Cipriani Hotel.

> 1 lb (450 g) fillet of beef, preferably Aberdeen Angus (fresh, not frozen)
> fresh rocket *or* arugula leaves — about 5 per person depending on the size
> 6–7 very thin slivers Parmesan cheese per person (Parmigano Reggiano is best)
> sea salt and freshly ground pepper
> extra virgin olive oil *or* Mustard Sauce (see below)

> *Mustard sauce*
> 2 egg yolks
> 2 tablesp. (2 American tablesp. + 2 teasp.) Dijon mustard
> 1 tablesp. (1 American tablesp. + 1 teasp.) sugar
> 2 tablesp. (2 American tablesp. + 2 teasp.) wine vinegar
> $\frac{1}{4}$ pint (150 ml/generous $\frac{1}{2}$ cup) light olive oil *or* sunflower oil
> 1 tablesp. (1 American tablesp. + 1 teasp.) grated fresh horseradish
> 1 generous teasp. chopped parsley
> 1 generous teasp. chopped tarragon

If you are using Mustard Sauce, make it first. Put the egg yolks into a bowl, add the mustard, sugar and wine vinegar and mix well. Whisk in the oil gradually as though you were making mayonnaise. Finally, add the grated horseradish, chopped parsley and tarragon. Taste and season if necessary.

Chill the meat. Slice the beef fillet with a very sharp knife as thinly as possible. Place each slice on a piece of oiled cling film, cover with another piece of oiled cling film. Roll gently with a rolling pin until almost transparent and double in size. Peel the cling film off the top, invert the meat on to a chilled plate and gently peel away the other layer of film.

Arrange the rocket leaves on top of the beef and scatter the very thin slivers of Parmesan over the top. Sprinkle with sea salt and freshly ground pepper. Drizzle with the Mustard Sauce or with very best extra virgin olive oil and serve immediately.

Note: Rocket and Parmesan Salad served without the carpaccio but drizzled with extra virgin olive oil is a very fashionable starter, and very addictive it is too.

Wine suggestion: A full bodied red, e.g. Sassicaia from Tuscany.

Crostini di Fegatini
Chicken Liver Croûtons

Serves 10–20

Crostini simply means croûtons and they are served in Italy with various toppings. Chicken liver crostini are the best loved in Tuscany. Recipes vary but I particularly enjoy this version which Mimmo Baldi served at his restaurant Il Vescovino in Panzano in the Tuscan hills.

9 ozs (255 g) fresh chicken livers

Mirepoix of vegetables
3 tablesp. (4 American tablesp.) extra virgin olive oil
1 carrot, finely chopped
1 onion, finely chopped
1 stick celery, finely chopped
3 anchovy fillets
$\frac{3}{4}$ oz (20 g) capers
$\frac{3}{4}$ oz (20 g) gherkins
1 stalk flat parsley
4 fl ozs (120 ml/$\frac{1}{2}$ cup) port *or* marsala
4 fl ozs (120 ml/$\frac{1}{2}$ cup) good homemade chicken stock
  (see *Simply Delicious 1*, p. 35)

salt and freshly ground pepper to taste

15–20 croûtons, $2\frac{3}{4}$ inches (7 cm) approx. toasted *or* fried in olive oil until golden brown on each side

Season the livers with salt and freshly ground pepper. Sauté the chicken livers in a little olive oil over a medium heat until they are just firm, remove from the pan and drain in a sieve or colander for 10 minutes.

Meanwhile prepare the mirepoix. Heat the olive oil in a saucepan over a medium heat, cover and cook the dice of carrot, onion and celery until soft — about 5–6 minutes. Add the chicken livers and cook for about 10 minutes more, then let this mixture cool for 30 minutes.

Add the anchovies, capers, gherkins and parsley to the livers and either mash with a fork or roughly blend in a food processor. Reheat this mixture, add the port or marsala and reduce until all the liquid is incorporated, then add the chicken stock. The mixture should have a moist creamy consistency. Taste and correct seasoning.

To serve: Just as soon as the croutôns are fried or toasted, spread with a generous amount of the fegatini mixture and serve immediately.

Mimmo likes to add a small tablespoon of chicken stock to each croûton just as soon as it is fried in olive oil. He then sprinkles them with a little Parmesan cheese, a generous amount of fegatini and serves them immediately — you always know when they have been served to a table because conversation stops and all one can hear is mmm, mmm!

Wine suggestion: A full-bodied red, e.g. Tignanello from Tuscany.

Deep Fried Courgette Flowers

Allow 1–2 flowers per person

Don't just glance at this recipe and say 'Is she mad?' If you grow courgettes you will of have lots of courgette flowers. They are edible and quite delicious — we tear them up and use them raw in green salad or in salades tièdes but you can also dip them in batter and deep fry them or, for extra posh, fill them with a stuffing and deep fry. They are different almost every time I do them, depending on what I have to hand, so you can experiment too. Goat's cheese, mozzarella and pesto is another of my favourite stuffings. Italians always use male flowers but you can use the female flowers and even deep fry them with the baby courgettes attached if you like.

12–16 courgette flowers (*or* **less**)

Batter (excellent for fish fillets also)
5 ozs (140 g/1 cup) plain flour
1$\frac{3}{4}$ tablesp. (2 American tablesp. + 1 teasp.) olive oil
water
1–1$\frac{1}{2}$ egg whites
sea salt
sunflower oil for deep frying

First make the batter. Sieve the flour into a bowl, make a well in the centre, pour in the olive oil, stir and add enough water to make a batter about the consistency of double cream. Allow to stand for at least 1 hour.

Just before cooking, whisk the egg whites to a stiff peak and fold into the batter. Add salt to taste. Heat the oil in the deep fryer until very hot.

Remove the 'thorns' from the base of the courgette flowers and the stamens from the centre, dip in batter and drop into the hot oil. Fry on one side for about 2 minutes and then turn over. They'll take about 4 minutes in total (they should be crisp and golden). Drain on kitchen paper and serve immediately — just as they are or with Tomato Sauce (see p. 19) or Tomato Fondue (see p. 75).

Courgette Flowers Stuffed with Cheese and Tomato

For each courgette flower use:
$\frac{1}{2}$ oz (15 g) goat cheese (I use Cais Cleire) *or* **mozzarella**
1 teasp. Tomato Fondue (see p. 75) or Piperonata (see p. 76) — not
   too runny
batter (see above)

Make the batter as above. Remove the 'thorns' and stamens from the courgette flowers, put the lump of cheese and the Tomato Fondue or Piperonata into the flowers and twist the ends to seal. Dip into the batter and deep fry, then drain on kitchen paper. Serve one or two per person as a starter.

Wine suggestion: Light red, e.g. St Amour from Beaujolais or a crisp dry white, e.g. Pinot Gris from Alsace.

Chargrilled Red and Yellow Peppers

Serves 8

The sweet, slightly smoky flavour of roast or chargrilled peppers makes this summery starter one of my absolute favourites. In fact every now and then I roast lots of peppers and store them peeled and seeded in a glass Kilner jar with a few fresh basil leaves and lots of extra virgin olive oil. Then I can dip in whenever I fancy and eat them as they are, or use them in a salad such as Rocket and Roast Red Pepper Salad, or as an accompaniment to pangrilled fish or meat. Magical!

> **8 fleshy red peppers (preferably Italian *or* Spanish)**
> **8 fleshy yellow peppers (preferably Italian *or* Spanish)**
> **8 fresh basil leaves**
> **2 cloves of garlic, cut into very fine slivers**
> **extra virgin olive oil**
> **10–12 black kalamati olives**
> **sea salt and freshly cracked pepper**
> **8 salted anchovies* (optional)**
> **8 salted capers* (optional)**

*Buy salted anchovies and capers if you can find them — they are incomparably better than those preserved in brine.

Preheat the grill or better still use a charcoal grill. Grill the peppers on all sides, turning them when necessary — they can be quite charred.† Put them into a plastic bag to cool and seal the end — this will make them much easier to peel. Peel the peppers and remove stalks and seeds — don't wash. Choose a wide, shallow serving dish. Arrange the peeled peppers, add garlic slivers, some fresh basil and a good drizzle of olive oil. Scatter a few black olives over the top and anchovies and capers if using. Serve with Bruschetta as a first course.

†Alternatively preheat the oven to 250°C/475°F/regulo 9. Put the peppers on a baking tray and bake for 20–30 minutes until they are soft and the skin blisters.

Bruschetta: Slices of thick Italian white country bread toasted on each side, rubbed when hot with garlic, then drizzled with extra virgin olive oil (see p. 97).

Wine suggestion: A Breganze from the Veneto, such as Maculan, or a good Valpolicella. There's a lot of poor quality Valpolicella around, so look out for a good one, e.g. Le Ragose.

Egg and Cheese Dishes

Provençal Tomato and Basil Omelette

Serves 2

For years I have enjoyed flat Provençal omelettes inspired by a recipe from Roger Vergé's book *Cuisine of the Sun*. Really dark red ripe tomatoes and fresh basil are essential to the flavour.

>   6 fresh eggs, free range if possible
>   4 tablesp. (5 American tablesp. + 1 teasp.) extra virgin olive oil
>   4 large very ripe tomatoes, peeled, seeded and diced
>   (14 ozs/400 g approx.)
>   salt and freshly ground pepper and sugar
>   10 leaves fresh basil
>   1 dessertsp. (2 American teasp.) parsley
> $\frac{1}{2}$ teasp. thyme leaves
>   1 clove garlic
>   6–8 black olives (optional)
>
>   non-stick frying pan, 10-inch (25.5 cm) top, 9-inch (23 cm) base

Heat half the olive oil in a non-reactive saucepan, add the tomato and cook over a brisk heat for 15–20 minutes or until all the moisture has evaporated. Season with salt, freshly ground pepper and a good pinch of sugar.

Put the torn basil leaves and parsley in a bowl together with the thyme leaves and add the clove of garlic scored with the prongs of a fork. Whisk the eggs in a bowl, add salt and freshly ground pepper, add the chopped parsley, thyme, and basil, the garlic clove and the cooked tomato. Season with salt and freshly ground pepper.

Put the remaining olive oil in a non-stick frying pan on a high heat. When it is very hot, pour in the egg mixture and cook, moving the mixture and tilting the pan until the eggs have set evenly but are still creamy on top and golden brown on the bottom. Retrieve the garlic clove and discard. Put a plate over the top of the pan and turn over on to a warm plate. Drizzle a little olive oil over the top and scatter a few small black olives over it also. Serve warm or cold with a green salad.

Wine suggestion: A dry white wine, e.g. Saint Veran from the Maconnais.

Provençal Courgette and Basil Omelette

Serves 2

Follow the recipe above, substituting 12 ozs (340 g) coarsely grated unpeeled courgettes (zucchini), softened in olive oil, for the tomato.

Provençal Terrine with Tomato Sauce

Serves 10–12

This is one of my favourite vegetarian terrines — it's really a multi-layered omelette. Prepare all your ingredients first and then cook one layer after the other very quickly. It makes a sensational starter or main course for a summer lunch party. Vary the flavouring if you wish.

Courgette layer
12 ozs (340 g) courgettes, grated on the coarsest part of a grater and
    sprinkled lightly with sea salt
2 tablesp. (2 American tablesp. + 2 teasp.) extra virgin olive oil
3 eggs, preferably free range
1 tablesp. (1 American tablesp. + 1 teasp.) cream *or* milk
salt and freshly ground pepper
1 dessertsp. (2 American teasp.) freshly chopped annual marjoram
1 tablesp. (1 American tablesp. + 1 teasp.) extra virgin olive oil

Tomato layer
14 ozs (400 g) very ripe tomatoes, peeled, seeded and chopped
2 tablesp. (2 American tablesp. + 2 teasp.) extra virgin olive oil
salt and freshly ground pepper
pinch of fresh thyme leaves
pinch of sugar
1 tablesp. (1 American tablesp. + 1 teasp.) cream *or* milk
3 eggs, preferably free range

Olive layer
2 tablesp. (2 American tablesp. + 2 teasp.) chopped black olives
3 eggs, preferably free range
1 tablesp. (1 American tablesp. + 1 teasp.) cream *or* milk
1 dessertsp. (2 American teasp.) parsley
salt and freshly ground pepper
1 tablesp. (1 American tablesp. + 1 teasp.) extra virgin olive oil

Spinach layer
$3\frac{1}{2}$ ozs (100 g) cooked spinach (7 ozs/200 g raw spinach)
salt, freshly ground pepper and freshly grated nutmeg
3 eggs, preferably free range
1 tablesp. (1 American tablesp. + 1 teasp.) cream *or* milk
1 tablesp. (1 American tablesp. + 1 teasp.) extra virgin olive oil
1 oz (30 g/$\frac{1}{4}$ cup) grated Gruyère cheese

1 loaf tin, 9 inch (23 cm) x 5 inch (12.5 cm) x 2 inch (5 cm), lined with
   silicone paper

Accompaniment
Fresh Tomato Sauce (see p. 19) or Tomato Fondue (see p. 75)

First prepare all the ingredients.

Courgette layer: Heat the 2 tablespoons of oil in a frying pan and cook
the courgettes until soft but still bright green. Drain, whisk the eggs,
add the cream or milk, the freshly ground pepper and marjoram, and
the courgettes.

Tomato layer: Heat the 2 tablespoons of olive oil in a pan, add the chopped
tomato, season with salt and freshly ground pepper, a good pinch of
sugar and some thyme leaves. Cook until soft, very thick and concentrated. Whisk the eggs with the cream or milk, add the concentrated
tomato paste, taste and correct seasoning.

Olive layer: Whisk the eggs, add the cream or milk, the chopped olives
and parsley, season with freshly ground pepper and a very little salt.

Spinach layer: Cook the spinach if raw in 1 tablespoon of melted butter
in a frying pan until soft and wilted. Season with salt and freshly ground
pepper and a generous grating of nutmeg. Drain, press out every single
drop of liquid and chop finely. Whisk the eggs, add the cream or milk,
stir in the spinach, taste and add more salt and pepper if necessary.

To assemble: When all the preparation is done, cook the layers one after
the other. Heat 1 tablespoon of olive oil in a non-stick pan $8\frac{1}{2}$ inches (21
cm) wide. Pour in the courgette mixture, stir around for about 30–60
seconds until the texture is just like a softly scrambled egg, pour
immediately into the lined loaf tin. Continue with the other layers,
sprinkling the spinach layer with Gruyère cheese, and cover the top
with a piece of silicone paper. Cook in a bain-marie in a preheated
moderate oven (180°C/350°F/regulo 4) for 10–15 minutes or until set
— it should feel firm in the centre and a skewer should come out clean.
Allow to cool.

French Onion Soup

Salad Niçoise

Courgette and Basil Omelette

Gougère

Serve lukewarm or cold with hot or cold Tomato Sauce (see below), lots of crusty bread and a green salad.

Wine suggestion: A light red, e.g. Chénas from Beaujolais or a Côtes du Roussillon.

Tomato Sauce

Makes 16 fl ozs (475ml/2 cups)

A good tomato sauce is a marvellous accompaniment to all sorts of dishes besides Provençal Terrine. I find it invaluable to have in the fridge or freezer as a standby. Use it on pizza or with polenta, with courgettes or courgette flowers — and of course you have a pasta sauce in seconds.

1 oz (30 g/$\frac{1}{4}$ stick) butter
2 tablesp. (2 American tablesp. + 2 teasp.) extra virgin olive oil
1–4 cloves garlic, depending on taste, peeled and chopped
1 medium onion, finely chopped
2 lbs (900 g) very ripe tomatoes, peeled and chopped
   or **2 x 14 oz (400 g) tins Italian tomatoes, chopped**
salt, freshly ground pepper and sugar

Melt the butter, add the olive oil and toss in the chopped garlic. Cook for 1–2 minutes or until pale golden, then add the onion, cook for a minute or two before adding the tomatoes then season with salt, pepper and sugar. Cook fast for 15–20 minutes if you want a fresh tasting sauce, or more slowly — for up to 1 hour — if you prefer it more concentrated. Purée through a mouli légumes. Taste and correct seasoning.

Variations
Tomato Sauce with Basil or Annual Marjoram
Add 1–2 tablespoons ($1\frac{1}{2}$–$2\frac{1}{2}$ American tablespoons) freshly chopped basil or annual marjoram to the above.

Tomato Sauce with Balsamic Vinegar
Add 1–2 teaspoons of balsamic vinegar to the tomato sauce just before serving. It intensifies the flavour quite magically.

Creamy Tomato Sauce
Bring the tomato sauce back to the boil with or without the herbs and add 4 fl ozs (120 ml/$\frac{1}{2}$ cup) cream. Bubble for 1–2 minutes and serve immediately.

Cheese Soufflé

Serves 8–10

Well risen soufflés always produce a gasp of admiration when brought to the table. Don't imagine for one moment that you can't do it — a soufflé is simply a well flavoured sauce enriched with egg yolks and lightened with stiffly beaten egg whites. Soufflés are much more good humoured than you think and can even be frozen when they are ready for the oven. The French do infinite variations on the theme, both sweet and savoury.

> melted butter
> $\frac{1}{2}$ oz (15 g/$\frac{1}{8}$ cup) Parmesan cheese (Parmigiano Reggiano is best) — optional
> $1\frac{1}{2}$ ozs (45 g/$\frac{3}{8}$ stick) butter
> 2 tablesp. (2 American tablesp. + 2 teasp.)/1 oz flour
> $\frac{1}{2}$ pint (300 ml/$1\frac{1}{4}$ cups) milk
> 4 eggs, preferably free range
> 2 ozs (55 g/$\frac{1}{2}$ cup) Gruyère cheese, finely grated
> 2 ozs (55 g/$\frac{1}{2}$ cup) freshly grated Parmesan (Parmigiano Reggiano)
> pinch of cayenne pepper
> freshly grated nutmeg
> salt and freshly ground pepper
>
> 8–10 individual soufflé dishes, $2\frac{3}{4}$ inch (7 cm) diameter x $1\frac{1}{2}$ inch (4 cm) high or 1 large dish 6 inch (15 cm) diameter x $2\frac{1}{2}$ (6.5 cm) high

First prepare the soufflé dish or dishes: brush evenly with melted butter and if you like dust with a little Parmesan. Preheat the oven to 200°C/400°F/regulo 6 and put in a baking sheet. Melt the butter in a heavy bottomed saucepan, stir in the flour and cook over a gentle heat for 1–2 minutes. Draw off the heat and whisk in the milk, return to the heat, whisk as it comes to the boil, cover and simmer gently for 4–5 minutes. Remove from the heat.

Separate the eggs and put the whites into a large copper, glass or stainless steel bowl, making sure it's spotlessly clean and dry. Whisk the yolks one by one into the white sauce, add the cheese, season with salt, pepper, cayenne and a little freshly grated nutmeg, stir over a gentle heat for a few seconds until the cheese melts. Remove from the heat.*

Whisk the egg whites with a little pinch of salt slowly at first and then faster until they are light and voluminous and hold a stiff peak when you lift up the whisk. Stir a few tablespoons into the cheese mixture to lighten it and then carefully fold in the rest with a spatula or tablespoon. Fill the mixture into the prepared soufflé dish or dishes (if you fill them $\frac{3}{4}$ full you will get about 10 but if you smooth the tops you will have about 8). Bake in the preheated oven for 8–9 minutes for the individual soufflés or 20–25 minutes for the large one (you will need to reduce the temperature to moderate, 180°C/350°F/regulo 4, after 15 minutes). Serve immediately.

I usually run a washed thumb around the edge of the dishes before they go into the oven to help to get the 'top hat' effect when the soufflé is well risen.

*Can be made ahead up to this point.

Individual frozen soufflés can be baked from frozen but they will take a few minutes longer to cook.

Wine suggestion: Givry from the Côte Chalonnaise in Burgundy.

Gougère
Cheese Choux Puffs

Serves 10

A great speciality of Burgundy, this cheese flavoured choux pastry comes in many guises from tiny little cheese puffs to gougère as big as your fist — but my favourite is the cheese galette which can be cut into slices like a tart. Anne Willan gave us this version when she taught at the school, and very delicious it is too.

Choux pastry
5 ozs (140 g/1 cup) strong white flour
6 fl ozs (175 ml/$\frac{3}{4}$ cup) water *or* milk
pinch of salt
3 ozs (85 g/$\frac{3}{4}$ stick) butter, cut into $\frac{1}{2}$ inch (1 cm) cubes
3–4 eggs, preferably free range

4$\frac{1}{2}$ ozs (125 g/1$\frac{1}{2}$ cups) coarsely grated *or* finely diced Gruyère cheese

Egg wash
1 egg
pinch of salt

Topping
1½ ozs (45 g/⅓ cup) grated Gruyère *or* Parmesan cheese
piping bag and ¾ inch (2 cm) plain tube

Preheat the oven to 220°C/425°F/regulo 7.

Next make the choux pastry. Sieve the flour with the salt on to a piece of greaseproof paper. Heat the water and butter in a saucepan until the butter is melted, then bring to a rolling boil and take from the heat. (Prolonged boiling evaporates the water and changes the proportions of the dough.)

As soon as the pan is taken from the heat add all the flour at once and beat vigorously with a wooden spoon for a few seconds until the mixture is smooth and pulls away from the sides of the saucepan to form a ball. Put the saucepan back on to a low heat and stir for ½–1 minute or until the mixture starts to 'fur' the bottom of the saucepan. Cool for a few seconds.

Set aside one egg, break it and whisk it in a bowl. Add the remaining eggs into the dough, one by one with a wooden spoon, beating thoroughly after each addition. Make sure the dough comes back to the same texture each time before you add another egg. When it will no longer form a ball in the centre of the saucepan, add the beaten egg little by little, using just enough to make a mixture that is very shiny and drops rather reluctantly from the spoon in a sheet. You may not need all of the reserved egg — if too much is added the dough cannot be shaped. (Choux pastry dough should just hold its shape when it's piped.) Stir in the grated cheese.

Put the dough into a pastry bag with a ¾ inch (2 cm) plain nozzle. Pipe 2½ inch (6.5 cm) rounds well apart on to a wet baking sheet. Brush each one carefully with egg wash and sprinkle with grated cheese. Bake in the preheated oven for 10 minutes, then reduce the temperature to 200°C/400°F/regulo 6. After 25 minutes pierce the side of each with a skewer to let out the steam and continue to cook until crisp, brown and irresistible.

Gougères are best eaten warm, but they can be baked ahead and popped into the oven to warm through before serving. Choux pastry puffs up better if used immediately but it can be stored covered in the refrigerator for up to 8 hours before baking. Rub the surface with butter while the dough is still warm so it doesn't form a skin. We also get very good results by freezing the uncooked choux puffs and baking from frozen next day.

Cheese Galette

Serves 8–10

choux dough made as above but use milk *or* milk and water instead
of just water

10 inch (25.5 cm) tart tin, preferably with a removable base

Preheat the oven to 200°C/400°F/regulo 6. Brush the base and sides of
the tin with soft butter and dust with flour. Add the cheese to the
dough. Spread the gougère mixture flat on to the tin with a wet spatula.
Brush with egg wash and sprinkle on the grated cheese for the topping.
Bake in the preheated oven until puffed and golden — about 45
minutes — pricking with a skewer after 30 minutes to release the steam.
Cut into wedges and serve while still warm.

Wine suggestion: A chilled white Burgundy, e.g. Chablis, is traditionally
drunk with this.

Quiche Lorraine

Serves 4–6

The classic Quiche Lorraine contains cream, eggs and bacon but no
cheese. However, I like the flavour of the cheese in this dish — but if
you want to eliminate it you can. The basic custard can be used as a
basis for many other quiches. Mushroom with Thyme Leaves and
Parmesan; Smoked Mackerel or Salmon, or that French bistro favourite
French Onion Tart — all you need is a little imagination, but remember
not to make the mistake of using the quiche as a dustbin!

Shortcrust pastry
4 ozs (110 g) plain flour
2–3 ozs (55 g–85 g/$\frac{1}{2}$ – $\frac{3}{4}$ stick) butter
1 egg, preferably free range
pinch of salt
2-4 tablesp. (2–5 American tablesp.) water

Filling
1 tablesp. (1 American tablesp. + 1 teasp.) olive *or* sunflower oil
4 ozs (110 g/scant 1 cup) chopped onion
4 ozs (110 g) streaky rashers (green or slightly smoked)

2 large eggs + 1 egg yolk, preferably free range
$\frac{1}{2}$ pint (300 ml/1$\frac{1}{4}$ cups) cream *or* **half milk, half cream**
3 ozs (85 g/scant 1 cup) freshly grated cheddar cheese
    or **2 ozs (55 g/$\frac{1}{2}$ cup) finely grated Gruyère cheese**
1 teasp. chopped parsley
$\frac{1}{2}$ teasp. chopped chives
salt and freshly ground pepper

flan ring *or* **deep quiche tin, 7$\frac{1}{2}$ inch (19 cm) diameter x 1$\frac{1}{4}$ inch**
    (3 mm) high

Make the shortcrust pastry in the usual way (see p. 82) and cover and rest in a refrigerator for 30 minutes.

Line the flan ring or quiche tin and bake blind (see p. 85) in a preheated moderate oven, 180°C/350°F/regulo 4, for 20–25 minutes.

Cut the bacon into $\frac{1}{2}$ inch (1 cm) lardons, blanch and refresh if necessary. Dry on kitchen paper. Heat the oil and crisp off the bacon, remove and sweat the onions gently in the oil and bacon fat for about 10 minutes. Cool.

Whisk the eggs, add the cream (or cream and milk), herbs, cheese, bacon and onions. Season and taste. Pour the filling into the tart shell and bake in a moderate oven for 30–40 minutes or until the centre is just set and the top golden.

Serve warm with a green salad.

Fish

Moules Marinière

Serves 4

Curnonsky, France's Prince of Gastronomes, declared that Brittany is a paradise for *coquillophages*. Apparently that unpronounceable word means shellfish eaters. Ever since I discovered it I've been longing to use it but haven't managed to get my tongue around it yet! The legendary mussel dish, Moules Marinière, can now be found not only in this area but all over the world — anywhere mussels are produced.

> **4 lbs (1.8 kg/2 quarts) scrubbed mussels, weighed in their shells**
> **2 teasp. chopped parsley**
> **2 teasp. chopped spring onions**
> **1 teasp. chopped thyme leaves**
> **1 teasp. chopped chives**
> **$\frac{1}{2}$ teasp. chopped fennel**
> **8 fl ozs (250 ml/1 cup) dry white wine**
> **4 tablesp. (5 American tablesp.) Hollandaise Sauce**
>   (*see Simply Delicious 1*, **p. 18**)
>
> *Garnish*
> **freshly chopped parsley**

Check that all the mussels are tightly closed and wash well in several changes of water. Steam open in a stainless steel pan on a medium heat with the wine, herbs and spring onions. Take the mussels out of the pan just as soon as the shells open. Remove the 'beard' and one shell from each. They can be kept at this stage for some time, even for a day or two in the fridge, as long as they sit in the cooking liquid.

To serve: Heat the cooking juices. When boiling, add the mussels, allowing them to heat through but not to cook any more. Remove from the heat and stir in the Hollandaise Sauce. Serve at once in deep oldfashioned soup bowls, sprinkled with freshly chopped parsley.

Wine suggestion: Dry white wine from the Loire, e.g. Muscadet de Sèvre et Maine or Pouilly Fumé.

Roast Monkfish with Bacon and Sage Butter Sauce

Serves 4

Monkfish, which used to be known as the poor man's lobster, is at last appreciated in its own right — and as a result the price has risen considerably, particularly on the Continent. Here it is roast and served with a sage-flavoured beurre blanc. The basic sauce without the sage is one of the great French classic emulsion sauces which makes virtually every fish into a feast.

> **1 x 16 oz (450 g) monkfish tail, trimmed of all membrane**
> **4 leaves of sage *or* 1 teasp. annual marjoram leaves**
> **6–8 thin slices streaky bacon, rind removed**
> **2–3 tablesp. (2–4 American tablesp.) extra virgin olive oil**
> **freshly ground pepper**

> *Sage Butter Sauce*
> **3 tablesp. (4 American tablesp.) dry white wine**
> **3 tablesp. (4 American tablesp.) white wine vinegar**
> **1 tablesp. (1 American tablesp. + 1 teasp.) finely chopped shallots**
> **pinch of ground white pepper**
> **1 generous tablesp. (1 American tablesp. + 1 teasp.) cream**
> **6 ozs (170 g/1½ sticks) unsalted butter**
> **2 sage leaves *or* 1–2 teasp. annual marjoram**
> **salt**

Put two sage leaves on top and two underneath the monkfish tail. Season with freshly ground pepper. Stretch the rashers with a knife and wrap around the fish, overlapping slightly as you go. Drizzle olive oil over the top, cover and leave in the refrigerator until ready to cook.

Preheat the oven to 250°C/475°F/regulo 9. Roast the fish for 25–30 minutes or until it is cooked and the bacon nice and crisp — it may be necessary to cover it two-thirds of the way through cooking time, or if you feel that it is cooking too fast turn the temperature down to 200°C/400°F/regulo 6. Meanwhile make the Sage Butter Sauce.

Boil the first four sauce ingredients down to about ½ tablespoon. Add the cream and boil again until it begins to thicken. Reduce the temperature to very low. Whisk in the butter in pieces, making sure that one piece is absorbed before you add the next. Add the chopped sage or annual marjoram. Keep warm.

To serve: Garnish the monkfish with fresh sage or annual marjoram leaves and bring it to the table on a hot carving dish. Cut into slices through the bone and serve Sage Butter Sauce separately.

Wine suggestion: A dry white Loire wine, e.g. Sancerre or a sparkling Vouvray such as Château Moncontour.

Italian Seafood Salad

Serves 8

Seafood salad is possibly the most popular cold seafood dish around the coast of Italy. Every port has its own version and even though the content varies they are all tossed simply in a mixture of olive oil and fresh lemon juice. Tiny squid or calamare are also a favourite addition. In this recipe I've included some grilled red pepper, a dice of cucumber and a few black olives which are delicious if not very traditional.

Dressing
3 fl ozs (75 ml) extra virgin olive oil
1½ fl oz (37 ml) freshly squeezed lemon juice
½ clove garlic
1 tablesp. (1 American tablesp. + 1 teasp.) freshly chopped mixed
    herbs e.g. parsley, chives and annual marjoram
salt and freshly ground pepper

Salad
1 lb (450 g) cooked salmon *or* monkfish (*or* a mixture of both)
    cut into 1½ inch (4 cm) flakes *or* chunks
1 lb (450 g) prawns *or* shrimps, cooked, *or* a mixture of prawns and
    scallops
4 lbs (1.8 kg/2 quarts) mussels, steamed, opened and removed from
    the shells *or* 2 lbs (900 g/1 quart) mussels and 2 lbs (900 g/1 quart)
    cockles *or* clams
1 grilled red pepper (optional — see p. 15)
½ cucumber, seeded and cut into ¼ inch (5 mm) dice (optional)
8 whole black olives (optional)
1 tablesp. (1 American tablesp. + 1 teasp.) chopped parsley
salt and freshly ground pepper

Garnish
sprigs of flat parsley
lemon segments
a few whole prawns *or* shrimps

First mix all the ingredients together for the dressing, adding salt and freshly ground pepper to taste. Shake well to emulsify before use.

Put the fish and shellfish into a nice wide bowl, add the cucumber dice, squares of roasted red pepper and stoned black olives if using and season with salt and freshly ground pepper. Very gently toss the fish in a few tablespoons of dressing — just enough to coat lightly — and sprinkle with chopped parsley. Marinade for 1 hour.

Just before serving, garnish with large sprigs of fresh herbs, segments of lemon and a few whole cooked prawns or shrimps.

Wine suggestion: A dry white wine from Piedmont, e.g. Cortese di Gavi.

Tuna à la Niçoise

Serves 6

Tuna is a much loved fish both in Italy and France. Its texture is quite meaty but it's all too easy to overcook it. The secret is to treat it like a piece of steak and cook it medium/rare, and then it will be meltingly tender and delicious.

> **6 pieces of fresh tuna, $1\frac{1}{2}$ inches (4 cm) thick**
> **olive oil**
> **salt and freshly ground pepper**
> **$\frac{1}{2}$ Tomato Fondue recipe (see p. 75), flavoured with a little tarragon**
>   **instead of mint or basil**
>
> *Anchovy butter*
> **$1\frac{1}{2}$ ozs (45 g /$\frac{3}{8}$ stick) butter**
> **2 anchovy fillets**
> **squeeze of lemon juice**
>
> *Garnish*
> **flat parsley**

Drizzle the tuna with olive oil, season with salt and freshly ground pepper and leave to marinade while you prepare the other ingredients.

Next make the anchovy butter. Pound the anchovies, mix in the softened butter and add a squeeze of lemon juice. Make into a roll, wrap in tinfoil or greaseproof paper and chill.

To serve: Reheat the Tomato Fondue. Heat a pangrill and cook the tuna for a few minutes on each side — remember tuna becomes very dry and exceedingly dull if it overcooks so catch it while it is still medium/rare.

Spoon 2 tablespoons of hot Tomato Fondue on to each plate. Put a piece of tuna in the centre and top with a slice of anchovy butter. Garnish with a sprig of flat parsley and serve immediately.

Wine suggestion: A rustic red from the Midi, e.g. Côtes du Ventoux.

Meat

*Boeuf Bourguignon

Serves 6

In this country, stew is generally regarded as something you feed the family but not your honoured guests. Not so in France, where this recipe for the most famous of all beef stews, Boeuf Bourguignon, might be served for a special Sunday lunch or dinner with friends. After all it is not cheap to make: you need best-quality well-hung stewing beef and the best part of a bottle of red wine. As the name suggests it used to be made with Burgundy, but with current Burgundy prices I think I might settle for a good Beaujolais or a full-bodied Côtes du Rhône.

6 ozs (170 g) streaky bacon
1–2 tablesp. (4–8 American teasp.) extra virgin olive oil
3 lbs (1.35 kg) stewing beef cut into 2 inch (5 cm) cubes
1 carrot, sliced
1 onion, sliced
scant 1 pint (600 ml/$2\frac{1}{2}$ cups) full-bodied red wine —
    e.g. a Burgundy, Côtes du Rhône *or* even a Beaujolais
2 tablesp. (2 American tablesp. + 2 teasp.) brandy (optional)
$\frac{1}{2} - \frac{3}{4}$ pint (300–450 ml/$1\frac{1}{4} - 1\frac{3}{4}$ cups) homemade brown beef stock
    (see *Simply Delicious 1*, p. 46)
1 tablesp. (1 American tablesp. + 1 teasp.) tomato paste
1 bay leaf
1 sprig thyme
2–inch (5 cm) piece of dried orange peel
2–3 cloves garlic
salt and freshly ground pepper
roux (optional)
18–24 small onions, depending on size
1 lb (450 g) fresh mushrooms, cut into quarters

Remove the rind from the bacon and cut into $\frac{1}{2}$ inch (1 cm) cubes. Blanch and refresh if salty, then dry well on kitchen paper. Heat the olive oil in a frying pan, sauté the bacon until crisp and golden and transfer it to a casserole.

Turn up the heat so that the oil and bacon fat are almost smoking. Dry off the meat. Sauté it, a few pieces at a time, until nicely browned on all sides, then add to the casserole with the bacon. Toss the sliced carrot and onion in the remaining fat and add these too.

If there is any fat left on the pan at this stage pour it off, add the brandy, if using, and flame it, then deglaze the pan with wine, scraping the little bits of sediment on the pan until they dissolve. Bring to the boil and pour over the beef.

The casserole may be prepared ahead to this point. Allow it to get cold, cover and refrigerate overnight or at least for a few hours. The wine will have a tenderising effect on the meat, and the other ingredients will add extra flavour as the meat marinades.

Bring the casserole to the boil, add enough stock to cover the meat, add in the tomato paste, dried orange peel, thyme, bay leaf and the whole cloves of garlic. Season with salt and freshly ground pepper. Bring to the boil, cover and simmer very gently either on top of the stove or in a low oven, 160°C/325°F/regulo 3, for $1\frac{1}{2}$ – $2\frac{1}{2}$ hours, depending on the cut of meat used. The meat should not fall apart but it should be tender enough to eat without too much chewing.

Meanwhile cook the onions and mushrooms. Peel the onions — this task is made easier if you can drop them in boiling water for 1 minute, run them under the cold tap, 'top and tail' them and then slip off the skins. Simmer gently in a covered casserole with about $\frac{1}{2}$ inch (1 cm) of water or beef stock — they will take about 30–35 minutes depending on size. A knife should pierce them easily.

Toss the quartered mushrooms a few at a time in a little olive oil in a hot pan and season with salt and freshly ground pepper. Keep aside. When the meat is tender, pour the contents of the casserole into a strainer placed over a saucepan. Discard the herbs, sliced carrot, onion and orange peel. Return the meat to the casserole with the onions and mushrooms. Remove the fat from the liquid. There should be about 1 pint (600 ml/$2\frac{1}{2}$ cups) sauce.

Taste, bring back to the boil and simmer. If the sauce is too thin or too weak, reduce for a few minutes, otherwise thicken slightly by whisking in a little roux. Pour over the meat, mushrooms and onions, bring back to the boil, simmer for a few minutes until heated through, and correct seasoning if necessary. Sprinkle with chopped parsley and serve.

Boeuf Bourguignon may be made a few days ahead and the flavour even improves with keeping for a day or two.

Wine suggestion: A full-bodied red Burgundy, e.g. Aloxe-Corton or Mercurey.

Fillet of Beef with Pizzaiola Sauce

Serves 4–6

In Italy there are several recipes for beef slices. Usually they use cuts like chuck and cook it in the sauce, but the result can be very tough so I have adapted the recipes and used fillet of beef.

> 1 lb (450 g) fillet steak
> salt and freshly ground pepper
> 3 tablesp. (4 American tablesp.) olive oil
> 3 cloves garlic, peeled and sliced
> 1½ lbs (675 g) very ripe tomatoes, peeled and chopped
> salt, freshly ground pepper and sugar
> 1 tablesp. (1 American tablesp. + 1 teasp.) freshly chopped basil *or*
>   annual marjoram

Heat the oil in a pan, add the sliced garlic and cook for a minute or so until it begins to turn pale gold. Add the chopped tomatoes and season with salt, freshly ground pepper and sugar. Cook for 4–5 minutes, add the marjoram or basil, taste and correct seasoning.*

Slice the fillet steak into ½-inch (1 cm) slices, season with salt and freshly ground pepper. Heat a wide frying pan and add a tiny dash of olive oil. Cook the steaks quickly on a very hot pan — they should still be pink in the centre. Pour the hot sauce into the pan and allow to bubble up for just a minute or two. Serve immediately on a hot serving dish.

*Can be made ahead to this point.

Variations

Fillet of Beef all' Arrabbiata
Add 1 red chilli to the tomato for a slightly fiercer but very delicious sauce, and remove before serving.

Fillet of Beef alla Sorrentina
Soften 4 ozs (110 g) sliced onion in the olive oil before adding the tomatoes and add 12 stoned black olives to the sauce at the end.

Wine suggestion: A full bodied red wine, e.g. Vino Nobile di Montepulciano or Tignanello, both from Tuscany.

*Pork Roast with Rosemary and Sage

Serves 10–12

Sage and rosemary, both strongly flavoured herbs, are great favourites in Italian cooking, particularly in Tuscany. Pork is usually roast without its skin, but you could score the skin and cook it separately if you want to have the best of both worlds.

> $4\frac{1}{2}$ lbs (2.02 kg) boneless loin of pork, without rind
> 4 large cloves garlic, crushed
> 12 juniper berries, crushed
> sprigs of fresh sage and rosemary
> salt and freshly ground pepper
>
> cotton string
>
> *Gravy*
> 1 pint (600 ml/$2\frac{1}{2}$ cups) homemade chicken stock (see *Simply Delicious 1*, p. 35)
> a little roux (optional)
> salt and freshly ground pepper
> a few knobs of butter (optional)

Open out the pork, season with salt and freshly ground pepper, spread the crushed garlic over the bottom streaky part of the loin and sprinkle with crushed juniper berries. Put 2 large sprigs of sage and 1 of rosemary in the centre and roll up tightly.

Arrange sage leaves and rosemary sprigs all over the surface fat of the meat and tie with cotton string into a neat sausage shape. Preheat the oven to 180°C/350°F/regulo 4. Roast for $2\frac{1}{2}$ – 3 hours on a wire rack until the juices run clear. Remove the joint of pork to a carving dish and allow to rest while you make the gravy.

To make the gravy: Degrease the juices in the roasting tin, add stock, bring to the boil and whisk to dissolve the caramelised juices on the roasting tin. Thicken with a little roux if desired. Just before serving whisk in some knobs of butter to enrich the gravy.

Wine suggestion: Dry white wine, e.g. a Riesling from the Alto Adige such as Renano.

Cassoulet
French Bean Stew

Serves 8

I am one of Elizabeth David's greatest fans, but it took me years to gather up the courage to try cassoulet after I had read and reread the descriptions of different types in *French Provincial Cooking*. My mouth watered — I longed to try this most comforting of winter stews — but I felt I would never manage to get all those ingredients together at one time. Eventually I plucked up the courage to try and realised that it's really just a bean stew. At its most basic it can consist simply of sausage and beans and everything else one adds in is a bonus. It also reheats very well and unless it's my imagination it gets better and better.

$1\frac{1}{2}$ lbs (675 g) haricot beans
1 carrot
1 onion studded with 2 cloves
bouquet garni
$\frac{1}{2}$ lb (225 g) streaky bacon *or* pickled pork
3 tablesp. (4 American tablesp.) olive oil
3 onions, sliced
5 cloves garlic, crushed
6–8 very ripe tomatoes
bouquet garni
2 pints (1.1 L/5 cups) homemade chicken stock
   (see *Simply Delicious 1*, p. 35)
4 legs of confit de canard *or* 2 pieces of confit d'oie *or* 4 fresh duck legs
1 lb (450 g) shoulder of lamb, cut into 4 thick chops
$\frac{3}{4}$ –1 lb (340–450 g) coarse pork sausages (quantity will depend on
   how strong the sausage is) e.g. Polish sausage, Italian Zampone
   or Cotechino, or Saucisson de Toulouse. Gelder sausage and
   coarse Bratwurst are widely available here* and we found a
   mixture of both very good.
2 ozs (55 g) white breadcrumbs

Garnish
chopped parsley

* Contact Horgan's Delicatessen, Mitchelstown, Co. Cork, tel. (025) 24977 to find your nearest supplier.

Soak the beans overnight in plenty of cold water. Next day cover with fresh water, add the carrot, clove-studded onion and bouquet garni. Cover and cook for $\frac{1}{2}$–$\frac{3}{4}$ hour or until the beans are three-quarters cooked. Drain.

Boeuf Bourguignon

Pork Roast with Rosemary and Sage

Chicken Roast with Whole Cloves of Garlic

Grilled Duck Breast with Caramelised Apples

Duck Legs with Onions and Thyme Leaves

Meanwhile, cut the bacon into 1-inch (2.5 cm) squares. Heat the olive oil in a casserole, add the bacon and fry until beginning to turn golden, add the sliced onions, garlic, peeled and sliced tomatoes, salt, freshly ground pepper and a bouquet garni. Cook for a minute or two, add the stock and allow to simmer for 15 minutes.

Remove the bouquet garni, then add the duck or goose confit, the shoulder of lamb, the sausage and finally put the beans on top. Bring the cassoulet to the boil, then spread a layer of breadcrumbs over the top. Put the pot into a slow oven, 150°C/300°F/regulo 2, and continue to cook for 1 hour or so until the beans and meat are fully cooked. By this time a crust will have formed and the beans will have absorbed most of the stock; if they haven't, remove the lid from the saucepan and cook uncovered for a further 15 minutes or so.

Sprinkle with chopped parsley and serve from the casserole (if you have cooked it in an earthenware pot all the better). Serve with a good green salad.

Wine suggestion: Red Hermitage or Crozes-Hermitage from the Rhône Valley.

Rabbit or Chicken with Mustard and Sage Leaves

Serves 6

Many French country people rear their own rabbits in hutches either beside or in their farmhouses. This recipe brings back memories of delicious rabbit stews I ate with Mamie and Papi Vienot in Lille sur le Doube. I have a feeling that many of you may be a bit squeamish about eating rabbit, but this recipe is also delicious made with chicken.

1 nice rabbit about $2\frac{1}{2}$ – 3 lbs (1.1–1.35 kgs) *or* 1 chicken
6 fresh sage leaves
2 teasp. mustard powder
2 teasp. grainy mustard, e.g. Moutarde de Meaux
4 fl ozs (120 ml/$\frac{1}{2}$ cup) dry white wine
$\frac{1}{2}$ oz (15 g/$\frac{1}{8}$ stick) butter
1 dessertsp. (2 American teasp.) oil
salt and freshly ground pepper
1 tablesp. (1 American tablesp. + 1 teasp.) wine vinegar
18 baby onions
8 fl ozs (250 ml/1 cup) crème fraîche *or* fresh cream and lemon juice
a little roux (optional)

Garnish
fresh sage leaves

Cut the rabbit into portions. Put into a terrine with the chopped sage leaves. Mix half the mustard powder and half the grainy mustard with 2 fl ozs (50 ml) water. Pour this and the wine over the rabbit and leave to marinade for about 1 hour.

Drain the rabbit pieces and dry them well. Put the butter and oil into a wide sauté pan and lightly brown the rabbit on all sides, then remove to a casserole. Degrease the pan, deglaze with the vinegar and pour this and the marinade on to the rabbit. Add the baby onions and the rest of the mustard. Add another 2 fl ozs (50 ml) water and salt and stir well. Cover and leave to cook on a gentle heat for 1 hour approx.

When the rabbit is cooked, take out the pieces and arrange on a hot plate with the onions (making sure the onions are fully cooked). Degrease, add the cream to the pot and reduce on a high heat until it thickens, whisking in a little roux if necessary. Taste and sharpen with lemon juice if needed. Pour the sauce over the rabbit pieces — through a sieve if you prefer a smoother sauce. Decorate with the rest of the sage leaves and serve immediately.

Wine suggestion: Pouilly Fuissé from Burgundy or Gewürztraminer from Alsace.

Chicken Breasts with Parmesan

Serves 6

This recipe is simplicity itself. It's also delicious if you smear a little mustard over the chicken breasts before covering them with cheese. You might like to drizzle a little cream on top too for extra wickedness!

6 boneless chicken breasts
milk
$2\frac{1}{2}$ – 3 ozs (70–85 g/generous $\frac{1}{2}$ – $\frac{3}{4}$ cup) freshly grated Parmesan
    cheese (Parmigiano Reggiano is best)
1–$1\frac{1}{2}$ ozs (30–45 g/$\frac{1}{4}$ – $\frac{3}{8}$ stick) melted butter

Soak the chicken breasts in milk overnight — this will make them wonderfully tender and juicy. Next day drain and dry on kitchen paper. Preheat the oven to 230°C/450°F/regulo 8.

Brush an ovenproof dish with a little melted butter. Season the chicken breasts and arrange in a single layer. Cover with Parmesan cheese. Bake in the preheated oven for 20–30 minutes or until golden on top and just cooked through in the centre.

Serve immediately with Piperonata (see p. 76) and a good green salad.

Wine suggestion: Italian Chardonnay.

*Chicken Roast with Whole Cloves of Garlic

Serves 4–6

If you ask what ingredient immediately springs to mind when French food is mentioned, the spontaneous reply of many people will be garlic. We often start by using it timidly, perhaps rubbing a cut clove over the salad bowl just to give a hint of garlic to a salad, but garlic has many different flavours depending on how you use it. Here we go to the other extreme and seemingly throw caution to the wind, roasting our chicken with lots and lots of plump garlic cloves. They will cook long and slowly and the flavour of the garlic will be transformed to a mellow sweetness which is quite addictive.

> 1 free range chicken, $3\frac{1}{2}$ – 4 lbs (1.57–1.8 kg)
> 1 sprig of thyme
> 2 ozs (55 g) peeled plump garlic cloves
> 1 lb (450 g) unpeeled plump garlic cloves
> salt and freshly ground pepper
> $\frac{1}{2}$ oz (15 g/$\frac{1}{8}$ stick) soft butter
> a good drizzle of olive oil
>
> *Gravy*
> 15 fl ozs (450 ml/$1\frac{3}{4}$ cups) homemade chicken stock (see *Simply Delicious 1*, p. 35) *or* $\frac{2}{3}$ stock and $\frac{1}{3}$ dry white wine
>
> cotton string

Season the cavity of the chicken with the salt and freshly ground pepper, then put in the sprig of fresh thyme and the peeled garlic cloves. Smear the breast and legs with some soft butter, season with salt and freshly ground pepper. Truss lightly with cotton string.

Preheat the oven to 180°C/350°F/regulo 4. Put the chicken breast side down into the roasting tin and drizzle with a little olive oil. Roast for 30 minutes, then turn breast side up and continue to roast. After 15 minutes add the unpeeled garlic to the roasting tin — toss it in the oil and chicken fat and add a little more olive oil if necessary. Continue to roast until the chicken is golden and fully cooked. Watch the unpeeled garlic cloves to make sure they don't overcook — the garlic inside the skins should be soft and sweet.

When the chicken is cooked remove to a serving dish, surround with the unpeeled garlic, spoon out all the garlic from the cavity and test to make sure the cloves are cooked. I often find that they need a little longer, so I put them into a saucepan with a little chicken stock and continue to cook for 5–10 minutes more or until they are soft, then add them to the carving dish.

Meanwhile make the gravy. Degrease the roasting tin, add the home-made chicken stock to the juices, bring to the boil and whisk gently to help to dislodge and dissolve the carmelised juices on the tin. Taste and season with salt and freshly ground pepper. If you like, thicken slightly by whisking in a little roux but I usually serve it just as it is. Serve the gravy and whole garlic cloves with the chicken.

Wine suggestion: A good white Bordeaux, e.g. Château Carbonnieux or Château d'Olivier.

*Grilled Duck Breast with Caramelised Apples

Serves 2

There are many recipes for duck breasts — *magret de canard* — in France. The fashion is to serve the duck very rare, but I prefer to cook it to 'medium well' because I find that otherwise it can actually be tough and unpleasant.

> 2 duck breasts (use free range ducks if possible)
> salt and freshly ground pepper
> $\frac{1}{4}$ oz (8 g/$\frac{1}{2}$ American tablesp.) butter
> 2 shallots, finely chopped
> 2 teasp. sugar
> 1 tablesp. (1 American tablesp. + 1 teasp.) red wine vinegar
> 2 tablesp. (2 American tablesp. + 2 teasp.) calvados
> scant 3 fl ozs (75 ml/$\frac{1}{3}$ cup) cider
> 8 fl ozs (generous 200 ml/1 cup) homemade duck *or* chicken stock
> (see *Simply Delicious 1*, p. 35)

Caramelised Apples
1 eating apple — Cox's Orange Pippin *or* Golden Delicious
$\frac{1}{2}$ oz (15 g/$\frac{1}{8}$ stick) butter
2 teasp. sugar
juice of $\frac{1}{2}$ lemon
1 tablesp. (1 American tablesp. + 1 teasp.) calvados (optional)

To finish the sauce
$\frac{1}{2}$–1 oz (15–30 g/$\frac{1}{8}$–$\frac{1}{4}$ stick) butter

Garnish
flat parsley

Trim the duck breasts and score the fat, then season with salt and freshly ground pepper. Heat a grill pan and cook the duck breasts fat side down for 15–20 minutes until most of the fat is rendered out and the skin is crispy, then turn and cook gently on the flesh side until cooked to your taste.

Meanwhile make the sauce. Melt the butter and allow to foam, add the chopped shallots and sweat gently for 3–4 minutes. Add the sugar and allow to caramelise to a good rich brown. Deglaze the caramel with the vinegar, calvados and cider. Reduce by about half or until the sharp alcohol flavour has gone. Add the duck or chicken stock and reduce, tasting all the time until you have a rich well-flavoured sauce.

Meanwhile prepare the apple. Peel, core and cut into $\frac{1}{4}$ inch (5 mm) slices. Melt the butter in a non-stick frying pan, toss in the apple and cook gently for 5 minutes, add the sugar and allow to caramelise slightly. Add the lemon juice and calvados (if using) and allow it to become syrupy. Remove from the pan and keep warm.

To serve, cut the duck breast into thin slices, fan out on a hot plate and garnish with the caramelised apples. Swirl $\frac{1}{2}$–1 oz (15–30 g/$\frac{1}{8}$–$\frac{1}{4}$ stick) butter into the hot sauce, taste and correct seasoning, spoon carefully over the meat, garnish with flat parsley and serve immediately.

Wine suggestion: A Châteauneuf-du-Pape, e.g. Clos des Papes.

*Duck Legs with Onions and Thyme Leaves

Serves 2

This delicious recipe was described to me by John Desmond late one night after a delicious meal in his restaurant on Hare Island, just off Baltimore on the south coast of Ireland.

2 duck legs
very little oil
1 lb 5 ozs (590 g) medium-sized onions, peeled and cut into quarters
sea salt and freshly ground pepper
$\frac{1}{4}$ teasp. fresh thyme leaves

Preheat the oven to 250°C/475°F/regulo 9.

Season the duck legs all over with crushed sea salt while you prepare the onions. Heat a tiny drop of oil in a heavy casserole, cook the duck skin side down on a medium heat until well browned, then turn and brown on the other side. Remove the duck legs to a plate, increase the heat and toss the quartered onions in the duck fat until slightly golden, pouring off some of the fat if there is an excessive amount.

Sprinkle with a few thyme leaves, season with salt and freshly ground pepper, put the duck legs back in on top of the onions, cover and cook in the fully preheated oven for 1 hour approx. or until the duck is cooked through and the onions are soft and juicy. Check every now and then. Serve the duck legs on the bed of onions. Garnish with sprigs of fresh thyme.

Wine suggestion: A full-bodied French red provincial wine, e.g. Faugères from the south-east — all the rage in France, so look out for it over here.

Confit de Canard
Preserved Duck Legs

Makes 4

Confit is an almost exclusively French way of preserving. First the meat is salted and then it is cooked, long and slowly, in the fat. Originally confit was made to preserve meat, particularly goose and duck for the winter, but nowadays this essentially peasant dish has become very fashionable.

4 duck legs, preferably free range *or* 2 legs and 2 breasts *or*
   the equivalent amount of goose
1 clove of garlic
1 tablesp. (1 American tablesp. + 1 teasp.) sea salt
1 teasp. freshly cracked black peppercorns
a few gratings of fresh nutmeg
1 teasp. thyme leaves

1 crumbled bay leaf
2 lbs (900 g) duck *or* goose fat (see method)
1 bay leaf
2 sprigs thyme
parsley sprigs
6 cloves garlic, unpeeled

Cut the legs off the duck carcase.* The breasts can also be used for confit but you may prefer to use them for another recipe, e.g. Grilled Duck Breast with Caramelised Apples.

Rub the duck legs all over with a cut clove of garlic, mix the salt, pepper, nutmeg, thyme and bay leaf together, rub the duck legs with the salt mixture and put into an earthenware dish. Cover and leave overnight in a cold larder or fridge.

Cut every scrap of fat off the duck carcases — you will need about 2 lbs (900 g). Render the fat in a low oven, strain and keep aside.

Next day, melt the fat on a low heat in a wide saucepan. Clean the cure off the duck legs and put them into the fat — there should be enough to cover the duck pieces. Bring to the boil, add the herbs and garlic, simmer on a low heat until the duck is very tender (about $1-1\frac{1}{2}$ hours — a bamboo skewer should go through the thickest part of the leg with no resistance). Remove the duck legs from the fat. Strain it, leave it to rest for a few minutes and then pour the fat off the meat juices. When the duck is cold pack into a sterilised earthenware crock or jar, pour the cool fat over so that the pieces are completely submerged and store in the fridge until needed. Leave it to mature for at least a week. When needed, melt the fat to remove the confit.

Serving suggestion: Serve hot and crisp on a salad (p. 10), or add to the Cassoulet (p. 34), or serve simply with thickly sliced potatoes sautéed in duck fat and some Lentils du Puy (p. 71).

* The carcase can be used to make duck stock. Follow the beef stock recipe in *Simply Delicious 1*, p. 46, substituting the duck for the beef bones.

Wine suggestion: A good vigorous red wine, e.g. Corbières or Coteaux du Languedoc from the south-east.

Roast Shoulder of Lamb Stuffed with Olives

Serves 16-20

Monique Avril (wife of the vigneron Paul Avril) showed me how to make this delicious Provençal recipe on a sunny afternoon in Châteauneuf-du-Pape.

1 shoulder of lamb (8$\frac{1}{2}$ lbs/3.6 kg with bones and 7 lbs/3.2 kg without bones)

Olive Stuffing
6 ozs (170 g/1 cup) black olives, stoned
2 large cloves garlic, peeled and chopped
2 anchovies
2 tablesp. (2 American tablesp. + 2 teasp.) extra virgin olive oil

cotton string

Gravy
1$\frac{1}{2}$ pints (900 ml/3$\frac{3}{4}$ cups) made with lamb *or* chicken stock

Ask your butcher to bone the shoulder of lamb for you or do it yourself if you are handy with a knife. Use the bones to make stock for the gravy.

Put the olives, garlic, anchovies and olive oil into a food processor and whizz for a few seconds — just long enough to chop the olives fairly coarsely: it shouldn't be a purée. Score the fat of the lamb lightly, then put the meat skin side down on your worktop, remove surplus fat from the inside, spread the olive mixture over the lamb and roll lengthways, tying at regular intervals with the string. Sprinkle lightly with salt and roast in a preheated moderate oven, 180°C/350°F/regulo 4, for 1$\frac{1}{4}$ hours approx. This will produce lamb with a faint pink tinge. Remove to a carving dish and allow to rest while you make the gravy in the usual way (see p. 38). Carve at the table and serve with a little gravy, some Ratatouille (see p. 71) and Rustic Potatoes (see p. 74).

Wine suggestion: A good Châteauneuf-du-Pape, e.g. Clos des Papes.

Pizza

Everyone loves pizza. It seems to me that it has almost taken over from the hamburger as the universal fast food. It has the advantage of being nutritious, very varied and fun to put together, but the big problem is that the only pizza bases most people have access to are less than delectable. A far cry from the warm, crusty squares of pizza which I saw being popped into children's satchels every morning in a bakery in Bologna years ago. What a wonderful school lunch system those mothers had!

The best pizzas are always made with a yeast dough — and this is where people tend to become fainthearted. Don't do that on me! Let me get you over your fear of yeast and believe me, it will be worth it. Pizza dough is, after all, just a basic bread dough with a little extra olive oil, so master it and hey presto, you will be able to make not only pizzas with myriad different toppings but also lots of irresistible crusty breads.

Once the dough is made the fun begins. With one batch you can make several different pizzas, maybe a sfinciuni, a calzone and focaccia. A whole afternoon's fun out of one piece of dough! If there are children around they can make their own pizza faces. And if you run out of ideas, roll out the dough anyway and pop the bases into the freezer. You'll be glad of them another day.

*White Yeast Bread Dough for Pizza

Makes 6 x 10–12 inch (25–30 cm) pizzas

In my family everyone loves pizza but each one has their own particular favourite, so I usually divide the dough into six pieces and then I can use lots of different toppings and keep everybody happy.

$1\frac{1}{2}$ lbs (680 g/$5\frac{1}{4}$ cups) strong white flour
$\frac{3}{4}$ oz (20 g) fresh yeast *or* half the quantity of dried yeast
2 level teasp. (1 American teasp.) salt
$\frac{1}{2}$ oz (15 g/1 American tablesp. + 1 teasp.) sugar
2–4 tablesp. (2–5 American tablesp.) olive oil
$\frac{3}{4}$ pint (450 ml/2 cups) lukewarm water — more if needed

43

Mix the sugar and yeast with $\frac{1}{4}$ pint of the lukewarm water, stir and leave for a few minutes until dissolved. Add the olive oil and the remainder of the water. Sieve the flour and the salt into a bowl, make a well in the centre and pour in most of the lukewarm liquid. Mix to a loose dough adding the remainder of the liquid or more flour if necessary. Turn the dough on to a floured board, cover and leave to relax for 5 minutes. Then knead for about 10 minutes or until smooth and springy (if kneading in a food mixer with a dough hook, 5 minutes is usually long enough).

Put the dough to rise in a pottery or delph bowl and cover tightly with cling film. Yeast dough rises best in a warm moist atmosphere, e.g. near your cooker, on top of a radiator or in a fan oven turned to minimum heat with the door left ajar. Rising time depends on the temperature — in an average kitchen it will take 2–3 hours.

When the dough has well doubled in size, knead again for about 2–3 minutes until all the air has been forced out again — this is called knocking back. Leave to relax again for 10 minutes and then use the dough as you choose. I find it very convenient to pop a few rolled out uncooked pizza bases into the freezer. You can take one out, put the topping on and slide it straight into the oven. What could be simpler!

This dough also makes delicious white yeast bread which we shape into rolls, loaves and plaits.

How to Cook Pizzas and Get a Well Browned Bottom!

I experimented a lot with my ovens to get the best result or at least the result that I'm happy with and I found I had to cook a different way in each oven. For all types of oven, preheat well ahead to maximum temperature — 250°C/475°F/regulo 9. In one of the electric ovens which has elements in the base and top of the oven I slide the pizza from the paddle directly on to the floor of the oven* — a 10–12 inch (25.5–30.5 cm) pizza $\frac{1}{8}$ – $\frac{1}{4}$ inch thick (3–5 mm) has a crusty base and bubbly golden top in 10–12 minutes.

In a fan oven, I put in a wire rack and cover it with four 8 x 8 inch (20.5 cm) quarry tiles which I preheat for at least 20 minutes. This gives an excellent result in a similar length of time.

In my 48-year-old Aga, which is my best friend, I preheat the baking sheet in the centre of the hot oven and slide the pizza directly on to it. Heat varies from Aga to Aga so some people may find it better to cook lower down in the oven.

In gas ovens or electric ovens with elements at the sides, I get best results by preheating the baking sheet in the oven on a high shelf and then proceeding in the usual way.

(*Since I filmed this television series, I have discovered that most manu-facturers do not recommend cooking anything on the floor of the oven. Check with your manufacturer: if in doubt perhaps a preheated baking sheet would be a wiser option.)

Pizza Paddle

The advantage of a pizza paddle is that one can slide the pizza with a flick of the wrist off the paddle directly on to a preheated baking sheet or bricks in your oven.

You can sometimes buy pizza paddles in kitchen shops, but if you can't lay your hands on one it's really easy to make it from $\frac{3}{8}$ inch (9 mm) plywood. The ones I use are 12 inches (20.5 cm) with a handle, so if you have an electric jigsaw you will be able to cut it out in a few minutes. However, it's essential to spend some time sanding and tapering off the edges so that the pizza can slide easily.

I discovered a great trick a few years ago. I now sprinkle the surface of the paddle with coarse semolina and put the pizza on top, and of course because the texture of the semolina is so gritty the pizza slides off into the oven with the greatest of ease. The pizza paddle can also be used to get the pizza out of the oven when it's fully baked.

*Pizza with Caramelised Onions, Blue Cheese and Rosemary

Makes 1

Serves 1–2

This is one of my great favourites, but it does take a little longer to make than some of the others.

> $\frac{1}{6}$ recipe for white yeast dough (see p. 43) — 7 ozs (200 g) dough
> approx.
> 4 onions, thinly sliced
> 2–3 tablesp. (2–4 American tablesp.) olive oil
> $1\frac{1}{2}$–2 ozs (45 g) Gorgonzola or Cashel Blue cheese
> 1 teasp. finely chopped fresh rosemary
> semolina if using pizza paddle (see above)

First make the caramelised onions because they take a long time to cook. (They are so delicious with steaks or even on toast that it's worth cooking 2–3 times the recipe and keeping them in the fridge.) Heat the olive oil in a heavy saucepan, toss in the onions and cook over a low heat for whatever length of time it takes for them to soften and caramelise to a golden brown — 30–45 minutes approx.

Preheat the oven to 250°C/475°F/regulo 9. Roll out the dough as thinly as possible into a round 10–12 inches (25.5–30.5 cm) in diameter. Sprinkle some semolina on to the pizza paddle and place the dough on top. Cover the surface of the dough to within $\frac{3}{4}$ inch (2 cm) of the edge with caramelised onions. Crumble the blue cheese and scatter over the top, then sprinkle with chopped rosemary. Drizzle with a little olive oil and slide off the paddle into the fully preheated oven. Bake for 10–12 minutes and serve immediately.

Wine suggestion: A Chianti, e.g. Brolio.

Pizza with Piperonata and Crispy Bacon or Salami

Makes 1

Serves 1–2

> $\frac{1}{6}$ recipe for white yeast bread dough, see p. 43 — 7 ozs (200 g) dough approx.
> 2 tablesp. (2 American tablesp. + 2 teasp.) Piperonata (see p. 76)
> 1 dessertsp. (2 American teasp.) crispy bacon lardons *or* 1 oz (30 g) salami, diced
> $1\frac{1}{2}$ ozs (45 g/scant $\frac{1}{2}$ cup) mozzarella cheese, roughly grated and sprinkled with 1 tablesp. (1 American tablesp. + 1 teasp.) olive oil
> semolina if using pizza paddle (see p. 45)

First preheat the oven to 250°C/475°F/regulo 9.

Roll out the dough as above and put on to the pizza paddle which has been sprinkled with semolina. Spread the Piperonata over the base of the pizza to within $\frac{3}{4}$ inch (2 cm) of the edge, scatter crispy bacon or salami over the top, sprinkle with grated mozzarella and oil and bake for 10–12 minutes. Serve immediately.

Variation
Substitute Tomato Fondue (see p. 75) for Piperonata.

Wine suggestion: A full bodied red Italian wine, e.g. Ghiaie della Furba.

Pizza Face

Makes 1

Serves 1–2

You can have great fun with pizzas. Children will love it if you put the ingredients on this one so that it looks like a face. If your children don't like some of the ingredients, substitute something else.

$\frac{1}{6}$ recipe for white yeast bread dough, see p. 43 — 7 ozs (200 g) dough approx.
2 tablesp. (2 American tablesp. + 2 teasp.) Tomato Fondue (see p. 75)
1 oz (30 g/$\frac{1}{4}$ cup) mozzarella cheese roughly grated and sprinkled with 1 dessertsp. (2 American teasp.) olive oil
4 anchovies
3 black olives
olive oil
semolina if using pizza paddle (see p. 45)

Preheat the oven to 250°C/475°F/regulo 9.

Roll out the dough as before. Cover the surface of the dough to within $\frac{3}{4}$ inch (2 cm) of the edge with Tomato Fondue. Sprinkle the mozzarella to resemble hair over the top and sides, arrange 2 olives for eyes and another for the nose. Make a wide grin with 2 anchovies and fill the centre with a little mozzarella. Make 2 earrings with the 2 remaining anchovies. Drizzle a little olive oil over the face and slide off the paddle in to the fully preheated oven. Bake for 10–12 minutes and serve immediately.

Wine suggestion: Chianti Rufina — or a glass of lemonade!

Pizza Margherita

Makes 1

Serves 1–2

Possibly the most traditional and universally popular pizza in Italy, it was apparently named in the last century in honour of Margherita, the pizza loving Queen of Italy. So there you are, now!

$\frac{1}{6}$ recipe for basic pizza dough, see p. 43 — 7 ozs (200 g) dough approx.

6 ozs (170 g/$1\frac{1}{2}$ cups) mozzarella cheese*

3 tablesp. (4 American tablesp.) olive oil

4 tablesp. (5 good American tablesp.) Tomato Fondue
   (see p. 75 — $\frac{1}{3}$ of recipe)

1 dessertsp. (2 American teasp.) freshly chopped annual marjoram

1 tablesp. (1 American tablesp. + 1 teasp.) Parmesan (Parmigiano
   Reggiano is best), freshly grated

semolina if using pizza paddle (see p. 45)

Preheat the oven to 250°C/475°F/regulo 9.

Roll out the pizza dough in the usual way.

Grate the mozzarella* and sprinkle with the olive oil. Sprinkle a little semolina all over the surface of the pizza paddle and put the pizza base on top. Spread the grated mozzarella over the base to within $\frac{3}{4}$ inch (2 cm) of the edge. Mix the freshly chopped marjoram through the Tomato Fondue and spread over the top. Sprinkle with the freshly grated Parmesan.

Bake in the fully preheated oven for 10–12 minutes or until the base is crisp and the top is bubbly and golden. Serve immediately.

Wine suggestion: A good Chianti Classico.

*The best mozzarella available in Italy, particularly around Naples, is made from the milk of the water buffalo. Its texture and flavour are sensational and quite different from the mozzarella made with cow's milk, *fior di latte*, and altogether different from the mozzarella available outside Italy. However, I have had great success with Marcella Hazan's wonderful tip to improve the flavour of mozzarella for cooked dishes. She suggests grating it on the largest part of a grater and then sprinkling it with olive oil — 1 tablesp. to every 2 ozs (55 g/$\frac{1}{2}$ cup), mix well and leave to steep for 1 hour.

*Sfinciuni

Serves 1–2

This speciality of Palermo is what one might call a pizza pie — it has dough on the top and bottom and a chosen filling in the centre. Again, there's nothing to prevent you experimenting but this is one of the many we enjoy.

$\frac{1}{6}$ recipe for white yeast bread dough, see p. 43 — 7 ozs (200 g) dough approx.

4 ozs (110 g/1 cup) roughly grated mozzarella cheese, soaked in 2 tablesp. (2 American tablesp. +2 teasp.) olive oil for 1 hour if possible

$\frac{1}{2}$ oz (15 g/$\frac{1}{8}$ cup) freshly grated Parmesan cheese (Parmigiano Reggiano is best)

3 tablesp. (4 American tablesp.) Tomato Fondue (see p. 75)

1 dessertsp. (2 American teasp.) freshly chopped parsley

1 dessertsp. (2 American teasp.) freshly chopped basil

2–4 anchovies and/*or* 6–8 stoned and halved black olives (optional)

semolina if using pizza paddle (see p. 45)

olive oil for brushing

Preheat the oven to 250°C/475°F/regulo 9.

Divide the dough in half. Roll out one piece as thinly as possible. Sprinkle semolina over the pizza paddle and arrange the dough on top. Mix the ingredients together and spread on the dough base to within $\frac{3}{4}$ inch (2 cm) of the edge. Dampen the edges with cold water. Roll out the remainder of the dough and put on top, seal and crimp the edges. Brush with cold water and slide into the fully preheated oven. Bake for 20 minutes or until crisp and golden. Brush with olive oil and serve immediately with a good green salad.

Wine suggestion: A good Chianti, e.g. Colli Fiorentini.

Calzone

Serves 1 very hungry person or 2 people who feel sharing is fun!

Calzone originated in Apulia, the high heel of Italy. Basically it is a covered pizza baked in the shape of a turnover or half moon. Again there are many fillings one can use. Here is one we enjoy.

$\frac{1}{6}$ recipe for white yeast bread dough, see p. 43 — 7 ozs (200 g) dough approx.

2 ozs (55 g/$\frac{1}{2}$ cup) crumbled goat cheese (we use Cais Cleire, but Lough Caum would be wonderful too).

2 ozs (55 g/$\frac{1}{2}$ cup) roughly grated mozzarella cheese soaked in 1 tablesp. olive oil if possible

1 teasp. finely chopped parsley

1 teasp. finely chopped annual marjoram
$1\frac{1}{2}$ ozs (45 g) cooked ham *or* crispy bacon
2 tablesp. (2 American tablesp. + 2 teasp.) Piperonata (see p. 76)
semolina if using pizza paddle (see p. 45)
olive oil for brushing

Fully preheat the oven to 250°C/475°F/regulo 9.

Mix all the ingredients for the chosen filling together. Roll the dough very thinly into a 12 inch (30.5 cm) round. Sprinkle the paddle, if using it, with semolina, put the dough on top and spoon the filling over the bottom half to within $\frac{3}{4}$ inch (2 cm) of the edge. Brush the edge with water, fold over the rest of the dough and seal the edge by crimping with your fingers. Brush the top with cold water and slide into the fully preheated oven.

Bake for 20–30 minutes. Brush with olive oil when baked and serve with a Rocket and Cherry Tomato Salad (see p. 80). (A steak knife is a good idea for cutting it.)

Wine suggestion: A good Chianti Classico, e.g. Castello dei Rampolla.

Pasta

I came across my first recipe for fresh pasta in *American Gourmet* about twelve years ago and I couldn't wait to try it. Day after day, sheets of pasta, noodles and pappardelle were draped over broom handles suspended between chairs, or dangling from the front bar of the Aga, and we ate pasta in every conceivable guise. I longed to go to Italy to see a real *sfogline* at work.

Eventually, at Marcella Hazan's cooking school, I watched fascinated as a woman stood rolling huge sheets of pasta with a four-foot rolling pin, using skill and rhythm which I found impossible to imitate. I was so intimidated that it put me off pasta-making for almost a year. Then I went back to my own method, forgot about trying to be rhythmic, and it works just fine.

When people first taste really good fresh pasta they feel it's sensational — and rightly so. However, it is worth noting that the Italians have no snob feelings about fresh versus good quality bought pasta. They use both types for different purposes.

There should be no mystique about making pasta. It's easier than pastry. The only time-consuming bit is the rolling out, but once you've done that you have a whole range of exciting options — from straightforward noodles to plump little cushions like cappelletti or tortellini.

Pasta machines for rolling and cutting are certainly a fantastic invention. (Mine has the added bonus that it can be either hand-cranked or electrically operated.) However, in my opinion the ones that mix the dough and extrude all sorts of different shapes are rarely worth the money, and can be tricky to work with different types of flour.

*Homemade Pasta

Makes 1 lb 5 ozs (590 g)

In Tuscany they make homemade pasta just with flour and eggs — no water and usually no salt.

> **14 ozs (400 g/scant 3 cups) plain white flour**
> **3–4 eggs, preferably free range**
> **1 teasp. salt (optional)**

Sieve the flour into a bowl and add the salt if using. Whisk the eggs together, make a well in the centre of the flour and add in most of the egg. Mix into a dough with your hand, adding the remainder of the egg if you need it. The pasta should just come together but shouldn't stick to your hand — if it does add a little more flour. (If it is very much too wet, however, it is very difficult to get it right.) Knead for a few minutes until smooth and then rest on a plate covered with an upturned bowl for 1 hour to relax.

Divide the dough in half and roll out one piece at a time into a very thin sheet, keeping the other piece covered. You ought to be able to read the print on a matchbox through the pasta. A long thin rolling pin is a great advantage but you can manage perfectly well with an ordinary domestic rolling pin.

Noodles, Tagliatelle, Fettuccine etc.

Allow the pasta to dry for 30 minutes approx. or until just dry to the touch, roll into a flat roll and slice with a chopping knife into whatever thickness you need. Open out and let it run through your fingers to separate the strands. Use immediately or allow to dry on a lightly floured tray.

Tagliatelle or noodles — $\frac{1}{4}$ **inch (5 mm) wide**
Fettuccine — $\frac{1}{8}$ **inch (3 mm) wide**
Pappardelle — $\frac{5}{8}$ **inch (15 mm) wide — cut with a pasta wheel**

Pasta can be flavoured and coloured in all sorts of ways. Add anything from tomato purée for orange pasta to squid ink for black designer pasta (the latter is not worth the trouble I assure you!)

Pasta Verde

5 ozs (140 g) cooked spinach ($\frac{1}{2}$ lb/225 g raw with stalks removed)
8 ozs (225 g/generous 1$\frac{1}{2}$ cups) plain white flour
2 eggs, preferably free range

Squeeze every single drop of water out of the cooked spinach, chop well or purée, add the spinach to the flour with the eggs and continue as for basic pasta dough. (You may not need all the egg.)

Pasta with Fresh Herbs

Mix 3 tablespoons (4 American tablespoons) finely chopped fresh herbs, e.g. parsley, chives, thyme, marjoram or a mixture with the flour and continue as in the basic recipe.

Tomato-flavoured Pasta

Add 2 tablespoons (2 American tablespoons + 2 teasp.) of tomato paste with most of the beaten eggs and continue as in the basic recipe.

*Tagliatelle alla Bolognese
Tagliatelle with Bolognese Sauce

Serves 6

Italians wince when we talk about Spaghetti Bolognese. They say there's no such thing — that Bolognese sauce should not be served with spaghetti but with tagliatelle instead!

> 1 lb (450 g) homemade tagliatelle or noodles (see p. 51)
> ragu recipe (see below)
> 1 oz (30 g/$\frac{1}{4}$ stick) butter
> 1$\frac{1}{2}$–2 ozs (45–55 g/generous $\frac{1}{4}$–$\frac{1}{2}$ cup) freshly grated Parmesan
>   cheese (Parmigiano Reggiano is best)

Bring 8 pints (4.5 L/10 American pints) of water to a fast rolling boil.

Heat the ragu, adding a little water if it is too thick. Add a generous tablespoon of salt to the boiling water and then add in the homemade tagliatelle or noodles. The pasta should be cooked within 30 seconds after the water comes back to the boil — taste a strand and as soon as it is *al dente* strain immediately.

Put a little sauce in a warm serving dish, top with the hot tagliatelle or noodles and pour the remainder of the sauce on top. Dot with butter, sprinkle with Parmesan cheese, toss well, and serve immediately with an extra bowl of Parmesan.

Wine suggestion: Dolcetto, a soft fruity red from Piedmont.

*Ragu
Bolognese Sauce

Serves 6

I've been told that if you want to make your way to an Italian man's heart it is essential to be able to make a good ragu. It is a wonderfully versatile sauce — the classic Bolognese sauce for Tagliatelle alla Bolognese, indispensable for lasagne and also delicious with polenta and gnocchi. I have been making Marcella Hazan's version for many years from her *Classic Italian Cookbook* (a book you would do well to seek out). It is the most delicious and concentrated one I know. Marcella says it should be cooked for at least $3\frac{1}{2}$ hours at the merest simmer and that 5 hours would be better, but I find you get a very good result with even $1\frac{1}{2}$ hours' cooking on a diffuser mat. Ragu can be made ahead and freezes very well.

> 3 tablesp. (4 American tablesp.) extra virgin olive oil
> $1\frac{1}{2}$ ozs (45 g / $\frac{3}{8}$ stick) butter
> 2 tablesp. (2 American tablesp. + 2 teasp.) finely chopped onion
> 2 tablesp. (2 American tablesp. + 2 teasp.) finely chopped celery
> 2 tablesp. (2 American tablesp. + 2 teasp.) finely chopped carrot
> 12 ozs (340 g/2 cups) minced lean beef, preferably chuck *or* neck meat
> salt
> $\frac{1}{2}$ pint (300 ml/$1\frac{1}{4}$ cups) dry white wine
> 4 fl oz (120 ml/$\frac{1}{2}$ cup) milk
> $\frac{1}{8}$ teasp. freshly ground nutmeg
> 1 x 14 oz (400 g) tin Italian tomatoes, roughly chopped with their
>   own juice.

> small casserole

In Italy they sometimes use an earthenware pot for making ragu, but I find that a heavy enamelled cast-iron casserole with high sides works very well. Heat the butter with the oil and sauté the onion briefly over medium heat until just translucent. Add the celery and carrot and cook gently for 2 minutes. Next add the minced beef, crumbling it in the pot with a fork. Add salt to taste, stir, and cook only until the meat has lost its raw red colour (Marcella says that if it browns it will lose its delicacy).

Add the wine, turn the heat up to medium high and cook, stirring occasionally, until all the wine has evaporated. Turn the heat down to medium, add in the milk and the freshly grated nutmeg and cook until the milk has evaporated, stirring every now and then. Next add the chopped tomatoes and stir well. When the tomatoes have started to bubble, turn the heat down to the very lowest so that the sauce cooks at the gentlest simmer — just an occasional bubble. I use a heat diffuser mat for this.

Cook uncovered for a minimum of $1\frac{1}{2}$ hours (better still 2 or even 3 depending on how concentrated you like it), stirring occasionally. If it reduces too much add a little water and continue to cook. When it is finally cooked, taste and correct seasoning. Because of the length of time involved in cooking this, I feel it would be worthwhile to make at least twice the recipe.

Spaghetti with Pesto

Serves 6–8

Pesto is the wonderfully fragrant basil sauce of Genoa in Liguria. The mere mention of the word whets the appetite and brings back memories of long hot summer days in Italy. It's worth growing basil just to make this one sauce alone.

> **1 lb (450 g) spaghetti**
> **2 heaped tablesp. approx. pesto (see below)**
> **freshly grated Parmesan cheese (Parmigiano Reggiano is best)**

Bring 8 pints (10 American pints) of water to a full rolling boil, add 1 generous tablespoon of salt, put in the spaghetti, stir well, bring back to the boil for 2 minutes, cover the saucepan with a tight fitting lid, turn off the heat and leave in the water for 10 minutes, by which time it should be *al dente*.

Drain the spaghetti immediately. Mix 2 tablespoons of the pasta cooking water with the pesto, toss with the spaghetti, sprinkle with freshly grated Parmesan cheese and serve immediately.

Wine suggestion: A dry Italian white wine — Frascati if you can find a good one.

Pesto

Besides tasting wonderful with all kinds of pasta and gnocchi, pesto tastes terrific with chargrilled polenta and a spoonful stirred into minestrone soup turns it into a feast. I even know people who are so addicted that they eat it on toast!

> **4 ozs (110 g) fresh basil leaves**
> **4 fl oz (120 ml/$\frac{1}{2}$ cup) olive oil**
> **1 oz (30 g) fresh pine kernels**
> **2 large cloves garlic, peeled and crushed**
> **2 ozs (55 g/$\frac{1}{2}$ cup) freshly grated Parmesan cheese (Parmigiano**
> **   Reggiano is best)**
> **1$\frac{1}{2}$ ozs (45 g/$\frac{3}{8}$ stick) butter**
> **salt to taste**

Whizz the basil with the olive oil, pine kernels and garlic in a food processor or pound in a pestle and mortar. Remove to a bowl and fold in the finely grated Parmesan cheese and soft butter. Taste and season.

Pesto keeps for weeks, covered with a layer of olive oil in a jar in the fridge. It also freezes well but for best results don't add the grated Parmesan and butter until it has defrosted. Freeze in small jars for convenience.

Pasta all' Arrabbiata
Pasta with Tomato, Chilli and Fresh Basil

Serves 4–8

This in one of the simplest and best loved Italian sauces. If you haven't yet discovered the excitement of cooking with chilli, you must buy some immediately and start to experiment. You can add real jizz to your cooking, but do it gradually!

> 8 ozs –1 lb (225–450 g) approx. spaghetti *or* spaghettini, depending on how saucy you like it
> 3–4 tablesp. (4–5 American tablesp.) extra virgin olive oil
> 2 large cloves garlic, cut into slivers
> 2 whole dried chillies
> 2 x 14 oz (400 g) tins good Italian tomatoes *or* 2 lb (900 g) very ripe tomatoes, peeled and chopped
> lots of fresh basil leaves
> sea salt, freshly ground pepper and sugar

Heat the olive oil in a wide saucepan, add the sliced garlic and cook for a few seconds, then add the chilli and the chopped tinned tomatoes. Cook on a high heat at first and then reduce to a medium heat for about 30 minutes. Season with salt, freshly ground pepper and add lots of torn basil.

Cook the spaghetti in the usual way (see p. 55). When the pasta is *al dente* drain well, toss in a little olive oil, season with salt and freshly ground pepper, then add the sauce, stir well and serve at once with freshly grated Parmesan cheese.

Variations

Pasta Pizzaiola
Cook as above but omit the chilli. Purée the sauce and add 1 teaspoon of freshly chopped marjoram and 2 tablespoons of freshly chopped parsley at the end of cooking.

Pasta Neapolitana
Proceed as above but substitute 2 teaspoons of freshly chopped basil for the marjoram.

Wine suggestion: A full bodied red Rubesco from Umbria.

Spaghetti with Mushrooms, Bacon and Parsley
Serves 4

This sauce can be put together in minutes and there are lots of variations depending on what you have in your fridge.

$\frac{1}{2}$ lb (225 g) spaghetti
2 tablesp. (2 American tablesp. + 2 teasp.) extra virgin olive oil
3–4 ozs (85–100 g) rindless streaky bacon, cut into $\frac{1}{4}$ inch (5 mm) strips
8 ozs (225 g) mushrooms, thinly sliced
2 cloves garlic, chopped
parsley, freshly chopped
salt and freshly ground pepper
fresh grated Parmesan cheese (optional)

Cook the spaghetti in the usual way (see p. 55). Meanwhile heat the oil in a frying pan, add the bacon and sauté until crisp. Remove the bacon to a plate but keep the fat, add half the chopped garlic to the pan, cook for a few seconds, then add half the mushrooms. Season with salt and freshly ground pepper and cook until the mushrooms are limp, remove to a plate and repeat with the rest of the garlic and mushrooms (adding more oil if necessary). Stir in the chopped parsley. As soon as the pasta is *al dente*, drain it, toss in a little oil or butter, turn into a hot pasta dish, spoon on the hot sauce, toss well and serve immediately either with or without some freshly grated Parmesan cheese.

Variations
Spaghetti with Mushrooms, Bacon and Marjoram
Substitute 1 tablespoon of marjoram for the parsley in the recipe above.

Spaghetti with Mushrooms, Bacon and Cream
Proceed as in original recipe but return the mushroom, bacon and parsley mixture to the pan, add 5 fl ozs (150 ml/generous $\frac{1}{2}$ cup) cream and allow to bubble for a minute or two. Taste, correct seasoning, pour over the pasta, toss and eat immediately.

Spaghetti with Mushrooms, Tuna and Parsley
Proceed as in the recipe above but omit the bacon and add in the tuna at the end.

Wine suggestion: A red wine, e.g. Ghemme from Piedmont.

Marcella Hazan's Pappardelle or Noodles with Chicken Liver Sauce

Serves 4

It was Marcella Hazan who first introduced me to classic Italian cooking and she has become a legend in her lifetime. This recipe is one of my favourites from her *Classic Italian Cookbook*.

$\frac{1}{2}$ lb (225 g) fresh chicken livers
3 tablesp. (4 American tablesp.) extra virgin olive oil
1 oz (30 g/$\frac{1}{4}$ stick) butter
1$\frac{1}{2}$ ozs (55 g) diced pancetta *or* prosciutto (I use unsmoked streaky bacon)
2 tablesp. (2 American tablesp. + 2 teasp.) chopped shallot *or* onion
$\frac{1}{4}$ clove garlic, peeled and finely chopped
1$\frac{1}{2}$ teasp. fresh sage
$\frac{1}{4}$ lb (110 g/$\frac{3}{4}$ cup) minced lean beef
6–8 twists freshly ground pepper
1 teasp. concentrated tomato purée dissolved in 4 tablesp. (5 American tablesp.) dry white vermouth
10 ozs (285 g) pappardelle *or* noodles — see p. 52

To serve
freshly grated Parmesan cheese (Parmigiano Reggiano is best)

Wash the chicken livers, trim off any fat or traces of green and cut them into 3 or 4 pieces. Dry thoroughly on kitchen paper.

Heat the butter and oil in a small saucepan, add the diced streaky bacon and fry gently until it begins to crisp, then remove to a plate. Add the butter and sauté the onions over a medium heat until translucent, add the garlic, stir 2 or 3 times, add back in the bacon and the sage leaves, then add the minced meat, crumbling it with a fork, and cook until it has lost its red raw colour.

Season with salt and freshly ground pepper, turn the heat up to medium high and add the chicken livers. Stir and cook until they have lost their raw colour, add the tomato purée and vermouth and cook for 8–10 minutes. Taste.

Meanwhile, cook the pappardelle or noodles until *al dente* in boiling salted water — 8 pints (4 L/10 American pints) to 1 tablesp. (1 American tablesp. + 1 teasp.) salt. If they are fresh they will only take a matter of seconds after the water comes back to the boil.

The moment the pasta is drained, transfer to a warm dish, add the sauce, toss thoroughly and serve immediately with grated Parmesan cheese if desired.

This sauce is also delicious served with Risotto (see p. 67).

Wine suggestion: A full-bodied Italian red, e.g. Barolo or Barbaresco, or Bricco Manzoni from Piedmont.

Lasagne Verde
Green Lasagne

Serves 12

Makes 2 dishes 11 x 8 inches (28 x 20.5 cm) or 1 large rectangular lasagne dish 14 x 12 inches (35.5 x 30.5 cm).

As a recipe, Lasagne has all the virtues — it is mildly exotic, suitable for large numbers, not too expensive and it can be made ahead and reheated very successfully. It's best made with homemade pasta verde but can also be made with good quality dry pasta. In my experience the no-cook lasagne benefits from being blanched and refreshed first, but whichever type you use, be particularly careful not to overcook it. Mushy lasagne is an abomination!

> spinach pasta (see Pasta Verde p. 52)
> 1 pint (600 ml/2½ cups) ragu (see p. 53)
> 2 pints (1.1 L/5 cups) well flavoured Béchamel Sauce
>   (see *Simply Delicious 2*, p. 20)
> 2½–3 ozs (70–85 g/½ – ¾ cup) freshly grated Parmesan (Parmigiano
>   Reggiano is best)
> a few knobs of butter

First prepare the ragu and béchamel sauce and set aside.

If using homemade pasta verde make it and allow to rest. Roll it out and cut into rectangular strips about 4 inches (10 cm) x 9 inches (23 cm).

Preheat the oven to 230°C/450°F/regulo 8. Bring a large saucepan of water to the boil (8 pints/4.5 L/10 American pints water to 1 tablespoon of salt), put in 3 or 4 strips of pasta at a time, stir and cook for just 30 seconds after the water comes back to the boil, remove and put into a bowl of cold water, then drain on a tea towel.

Taste each sauce to make sure it is well seasoned. Take one large or two small lasagne dishes, spread a little béchamel on the base, cover with a layer of barely overlapping sheets of pasta. Spread a little ragu on the pasta, just enough to dot it with meat (remember this is a very rich and concentrated sauce). Spread a layer of béchamel over the ragu, sprinkle lightly with freshly grated Parmesan cheese, then continue with another layer of pasta and so on up to within 1 inch (2.5 cm) of the top of the dish (don't make more than 6 layers). Finish with a layer of pasta coated with béchamel, sprinkle with the remainder of the cheese and dot with a few little knobs of butter.*

Wipe the edges clean. Bake in the preheated oven for 10–15 minutes — don't overcook — and allow to rest for about 5 minutes. Serve from the dish — it should be bubbly and golden on top.

*Can be prepared ahead to this point and kept in the fridge for several days or frozen for up to 3 months.

Variations
The lasagne technique can be used successfully with all sorts of fillings.

Lasagne with Ragu and Piperonata
We make a variation on the above by substituting Piperonata (see p. 76) for ragu in one or two of the layers.

Vegetarian Lasagne
You can make Vegetarian Lasagne with many different layers (see *Simply Delicious 2*, p. 76), but Courgettes with Marjoram or Basil (see p. 78) layered with a thick béchamel sauce and Parmesan make a particularly delicious vegetarian lasagne.

Wine suggestion: A light red wine, e.g. Bardolino from the Veneto area or a dry white wine, e.g. Bianco di Coltibuono.

How to Make Cappelletti and Tortellini

Serves 10–12 people

Makes about 300

Capelletti and tortellini are little stuffed pasta, very much a labour of love to make but quite delicious to eat. I was interested to discover that it is tradition to serve cappelletti in broth on Christmas and New Year's Day in parts of Emilia Romagna. On Christmas Eve the entire family from children to grannies become involved — everyone sits around the kitchen table and shapes the little dumplings. In fact children are often best at this because their fingers are small and nimble. By the time several hundred have been made everyone has had lots of fun and the skill has unwittingly been passed on from one generation to the next. This recipe, one of my great favourites, is adapted from *The Classic Italian Cookbook* by Marcella Hazan.

1 quantity of homemade pasta dough (see p. 51)

Filling
1 oz (30 g/$\frac{1}{4}$ stick) butter
4 ozs (110 g) pork fillet, cut into $\frac{1}{2}$ inch (1 cm) dice
6 ozs (170 g) chicken breast, cut into $\frac{1}{2}$ inch (1 cm) dice
$1\frac{1}{2}$ ozs (45 g) garlic salami
9 ozs (225 g/generous 1 cup) ricotta *or* sieved cottage cheese
1 egg yolk, preferably free range
$3\frac{1}{2}$ ozs (100 g/scant 1 cup) freshly grated Parmesan (Parmigiano Reggiano is best)
$\frac{1}{2}$ teasp. freshly grated nutmeg
salt and freshly ground pepper

First make the pasta dough, cover and allow to rest while you make the filling.

Melt the butter in a heavy-bottomed saucepan, add the diced pork, season with salt and freshly ground pepper and cook gently until nicely browned and cooked through. Remove to a plate, then add the diced chicken breasts to the saucepan, season again and cook — they won't take so long: about 2–3 minutes. Add to the pork. Allow to cool while you prepare the other ingredients.

Chop the garlic salami very finely and mix with the sieved cottage cheese, grated Parmesan and egg yolk. Chop the cooked pork and chicken very finely (you can do this in a food processor if you are very careful, using the pulse button, but don't let it reach a purée).

Add to the other ingredients, grate in the nutmeg, season with salt and freshly ground pepper, mix well, taste and add more seasoning if necessary. Cover and keep in the fridge until you are ready to make the cappelletti.

Divide the dough in half, cover one piece and roll the other piece into a very thin sheet. Repeat. Then cut the pasta into $1\frac{3}{4}$ inch (4.5 cm) squares for cappelletti or 2 inch (5 cm) rounds for tortellini. You will probably have to trim the edges quite a bit to get even strips and squares, but keep the trimmings. Cut them into noodles and you can cook them another time.

The dough for stuffed pasta should not be dried, so gather your helpers around you and set to work right away. Put the equivalent of $\frac{1}{4}$ teaspoon of filling in the centre of each square (do this with your fingers — it's much faster). Then fold the square in half diagonally to form a triangle, press down firmly to seal the sides, pick up the triangle by one end of its long base, hold it between your thumb and index fingers with the tip of the triangle pointing towards your knuckle, catch the other end of the base with your other hand and wrap it around your index finger, press the two ends firmly together to seal, then slide the cappelletti off your finger and push the little peak ends upwards so they resemble those wondrous bonnets worn by nuns years ago.

At this point I reckon it's worth the effort to pause and cook two or three in a little boiling salted water to check the flavour. Although it's great fun, this is not exactly fast food and nothing is more disappointing than to discover that they could have done with a little more seasoning when it's too late.

As you make the cappelletti, put them out on clean dry tea towels. You can cook them right away, but otherwise turn them every couple of hours until they are uniformly dry (in Restaurant Diana in Bologna they have a wooden frame with perforated zinc specially for drying the cappelletti). When they are dry they will keep for up to a week.

Wine suggestion: An Italian Chardonnay.

Cappelletti or Tortellini with Butter and Cream

Serves 8

> 150 cappelletti or tortellini (see p. 60)
> $1\frac{1}{2}$ ozs (45 g/$\frac{3}{8}$ stick) butter
> 5 fl ozs (150 ml/generous $\frac{1}{2}$ cup) cream
> $1\frac{3}{4}$ oz (50 g/scant $\frac{1}{2}$ cup) freshly grated Parmesan cheese (Parmigiano Reggiano is best)
> extra Parmesan for sprinkling

Bring 8 pints (4.5 L/10 American pints) of water to a fast rolling boil, add 1 generous tablespoon of salt and 1 tablespoon of oil. Drop in the cappelletti, stir gently and as soon as the water comes back to the boil time them: fresh cappelletti will take 4–5 minutes but dry cappelletti may take up to 20 minutes. Have a colander or large slotted spoon ready.

Meanwhile, melt the butter and cream in a wide sauté pan. As soon as the cappelletti are cooked scoop up and drain, add to the butter and cream, put on a low heat and toss gently in the sauce. Add the grated Parmesan cheese and continue to toss until they are evenly coated. Turn into a hot serving dish and serve immediately on hot plates with an extra sprinkling of Parmesan cheese.

Wine suggestion: A good Italian dry white wine, e.g. Pomino Bianco from Frescobaldi.

Taglierini al Profumo di Limone
Fresh Noodles with Lemon

Serves 6

This recipe was given to me by Mimmo Baldi, the chef-owner of Il Vescovino in Panzano. His restaurant overlooking many of the best vineyards in Chianti serves some of the most inspired food I have tasted in Italy — certainly worth a detour.

 7 ozs (200 g) fresh *or* dried taglierini (thin noodles)
 5 fl ozs (150 ml/generous $\frac{1}{2}$ cup) very fresh cream
 2 fresh lemons
 salt and freshly ground pepper to taste
 a knob of butter

Scrub the lemons gently to remove any wax, then grate the lemon zest on the finest part of a stainless steel grater, add it to the cream, cover the bowl and leave to infuse in the fridge for 5–6 hours.

Cook the pasta in plenty of boiling salted water until *al dente*, drain well and put into a hot pasta dish, adding the cream and lemon mixture. Season with salt and freshly ground pepper, add a knob of butter and toss well. Serve instantly. This sauce should not be thick.

Wine suggestion: A dry white Italian wine, e.g. Villa Antinori Bianco.

Risotto and Polenta

There's something very comforting about sitting down to a plate of creamy risotto with butter and Parmesan cheese melting over the top. Certainly risotto deserves to be better known and understood. Too often it is regarded as a way of using up miscellaneous leftovers of doubtful origin. The Italians would be appalled by this attitude to a classic Venetian dish which is treated with great reverence. It can be very simple or quite exotic, embellished with anything from seafood to *porcini*.

There are several secrets to a really good risotto. The first is the rice: you have to search for Italian *arborio, carnaroli* or *vialone nano*. The second is the broth which must be homemade, the third the cooking method and the fourth and most crucial is to eat the risotto at the precise moment when it is cooked but still creamy — not gluey and dry.

The vital finishing touch is freshly grated good quality Parmesan — *Parmigiano Reggiano*. Sadly, ready-grated Parmesan cheese is rarely a good buy and can often ruin a whole dish.

Polenta, which is to the Northern Italians what potatoes are to the Irish, is difficult to describe if you don't know it. The best I can do is to call it a porridge made with maize, but I wince at that indelicate description. I'm addicted to this steaming golden staple which brings a sparkle to Italian eyes.

I should warn you, however, that it's not necessarily something you will be hooked on at first taste. I well remember the first time I was introduced to it by an Italian friend, Ada Paraselitti. I had a mouthful and thought, my God, she spent 45 minutes stirring *that*! I now realise it's an acquired taste and my palate simply needed more education.

Polenta, once called *stramaledetta* (the cursed) and *il cibo della miseria* (the food of poverty) was peasant sustenance for three centuries, eaten for breakfast, lunch and dinner — but now it has become enormously trendy. The glorious thing is that it can be served in so many ways. Leftovers, sliced and pangrilled, can have so many different, delicious toppings such as caramelised onions and pesto, or rocket with tomato and marjoram. Do try it and you'll see what all the fuss is about.

*Risotto alla Parmigiana
Risotto with Parmesan Cheese

Serves 6

The rice dishes of the Veneto region are famous. Rice was introduced there by the Arabs and many varieties of short-grain rice still grow in the marsh lands around the river Po. In Venice, risotto is made almost liquid. Its great quality is its immense versatility. The Veneto is richer in vegetables than any other area in Italy, so all sorts of vegetables and combinations of vegetables are included in the dish as well as herbs, poultry, game, chicken livers or shellfish. There is even a risotto made with squid ink and another with pine kernels and raisins which is actually a legacy of the Arabs.

$1\frac{3}{4}$–$2\frac{1}{4}$ pints (1–1.3 L/$4\frac{1}{2}$–$5\frac{1}{2}$ cups) broth *or* chicken stock
   (see *Simply Delicious 1*, **p. 35**)
1 oz (30 g/$\frac{1}{4}$ stick) butter
1 onion, finely chopped
2 tablesp. (2 American tablesp. + 2 teasp.) olive oil
14 ozs (400 g/scant 2 cups) carnaroli *or* arborio rice
1 oz (30 g/$\frac{1}{4}$ stick) butter
2 ozs (55 g/$\frac{1}{2}$ cup) freshly grated Parmesan cheese (Parmigiano
   Reggiano is best)
sea salt

First bring the broth or stock to the boil, turn down the heat and keep it simmering. Melt 1 oz (30 g/$\frac{1}{4}$ stick) butter in a heavy-bottomed sauce-pan with the oil, add the onion and sweat over a gentle heat for 4–5 minutes, until soft but not coloured. Add the rice and stir until well coated (so far the technique is the same as for a pilaff and this is where people become confused). Cook for a minute or so and then add $\frac{1}{4}$ pint (150 ml/generous $\frac{1}{2}$ cup) of the simmering broth, stir continuously and as soon as the liquid is absorbed add another $\frac{1}{4}$ pint (150 ml/generous $\frac{1}{2}$ cup) of broth. Continue to cook, stirring continuously. The heat should be brisk, but on the other hand if it's too hot the rice will be soft outside but still chewy inside. If it's too slow, the rice will be gluey. It's difficult to know which is worse, so the trick is to regulate the heat so that the rice bubbles continuously. The risotto should take abut 25–30 minutes to cook.

When it is cooking for about 20 minutes, add the broth about 4 table-spoons (5 American tablespoons) at a time. I use a small ladle, and watch it very carefully from there on. The risotto is done when the rice is cooked but is still ever so slightly *al dente*. It should be soft and creamy and quite loose, rather than thick. The moment you are happy with the texture, stir in the remaining butter and Parmesan cheese, taste and add more salt if necessary. Serve immediately. Risotto does not hang around.

Wine suggestion: A dry white Soave Classico, e.g. Vignetto Calvarino.

Risotto con Ragu

Add $\frac{1}{2}$ pint (300 ml/$1\frac{1}{4}$ cups) Ragu (see p. 53) to the rice just before you add the broth, then continue as in the basic recipe. Taste carefully — you may not need all the cheese.

Risotto with Chicken Liver Sauce

Follow the basic recipe above and pour the risotto into a hot serving dish. Fill the centre with chicken liver sauce (see p. 58) and serve immediately.

Risotto with Dried Mushrooms

Serves 16

This is one of the very best ways to get maximum value from some precious expensive dried mushrooms.

> ingredients for basic Risotto recipe (p. 65) plus $\frac{1}{4}$–$\frac{1}{2}$ oz (8–15 g) dried mushrooms, e.g. porcini, boletus *or* cèpes, but you will need only 1 oz (30 g) freshly grated Parmesan cheese (Parmgiano Reggiano is best). Add freshly ground pepper.

Soak the dried mushrooms in $\frac{3}{4}$ pint (450 ml/generous $1\frac{1}{2}$ cups) of luke-warm water for 30 minutes, strain and filter off the dark liquid and save. Wash the mushrooms well to make sure there is no grit left.

Start the risotto in the usual way (see p. 65).

When the rice has cooked for about 12 minutes add the mushrooms and $\frac{1}{4}$ pint (150 ml/generous $\frac{1}{2}$ cup) of the strained liquid, continue to add the mushroom liquid until it is all used up and then revert to the simmering broth until the rice is cooked. Stir in the remainder of the butter and the Parmesan cheese. Taste, adding salt if necessary. *Serve immediately*. Serve extra Parmesan for sprinkling.

Wine suggestion: A dry white Italian wine from Colli Berici in the Veneto, e.g. Bianco del Rocolo.

(Clockwise from top) Calzone; Pizza with Caramelised Onions, Blue Cheese and Rosemary; Pizza with Piperonata and Crispy Bacon; Pizza Face

Pasta Preparation

Pesto Preparation

Chargrilled Polenta with **(clockwise from top)** Roasted Red Pepper; Olive Paste; Caramelised Onions and Pesto; Gorgonzola or Blue Cheese

Rocket and Cherry Tomato Salad

*Risotto Primavera
Risotto with Fresh Vegetables

Serves 6

Renato Piccoloto, head chef at the Cipriani in Venice, demonstrated this Risotto Primavera for us in the garden overlooking the lagoon. The flavour was quite exquisite — one mouthful and one could understand why the Venetians love their risotto so much.

$\frac{1}{2}$ oz (15 g/$\frac{1}{8}$ stick) butter
1 tablesp. (1 American tablesp. + 1 teasp.) olive oil
2 ozs (55 g) red pepper, peeled and seeded, cut into scant $\frac{1}{4}$ inch (5 mm) dice
2 ozs (55 g) French beans, cut into $\frac{1}{4}$ inch (5 mm) dice
2 small courgettes (zucchini) cut into 1-inch (2.5 cm) fine julienne strips
1 celery heart, 2 ozs (55 g), cut into 1-inch (2.5 cm) fine julienne strips
2 ozs (55 g) carrot, cut into 1-inch (2.5 cm) fine julienne strips
2 ozs (55 g) fresh peas
2 ozs (55 g) sliced porcini mushrooms or flat mushrooms, cooked in a tiny bit of butter
2 ozs (55 g) tomato, peeled, seeded and cut into $\frac{1}{4}$ inch (5 mm) dice
1$\frac{3}{4}$–2 pints (1–1.1 L/4$\frac{1}{4}$–5 cups) broth or homemade chicken stock (see *Simply Delicious 1*, p. 35)
1 oz (30 g/$\frac{1}{4}$ stick) butter
3 ozs (85 g/$\frac{3}{4}$ cup) onion, finely chopped
16 oz (450 g/generous 2 cups) risotto rice (Renato likes to use vialone nano but you can use arboria or carnaroli also)
2$\frac{1}{2}$ ozs (70 g/$\frac{5}{8}$ stick) unsalted butter
2$\frac{1}{2}$ ozs (45 g/generous $\frac{1}{2}$ cup) freshly grated Parmesan cheese (Parmigiano Reggiano is best)
sea salt

First prepare the vegetables. Bring the broth to the boil, melt the $\frac{1}{2}$ oz (15 g) butter with the olive oil in a heavy-bottomed saucepan, add the peppers, beans, courgettes (zucchini), celery and carrot. Stir for 2–3 minutes over a medium heat, then add the peas, mushrooms and tomato dice, cover and cook for 3–4 minutes — they should remain *al dente*. Remove from the pan on to a plate and keep aside for later.

Melt 1 oz (30 g) butter in a saucepan, add in the onion and cook until pale golden and tender, add the rice and stir until it is translucent, add about $\frac{1}{4}$ pint (150 ml/generous $\frac{1}{3}$ cup) of simmering broth (use a ladle) and stir all the time over a lively heat until the broth has almost been absorbed. Then add another ladleful of broth, continuing to stir, and when that is absorbed add more and so on.

After about 12 minutes, add back in the vegetables and continue to cook, adding more broth as it is necessary. When the rice is almost cooked add just a few tablespoons of broth at a time. The risotto usually takes 18–20 minutes to cook but taste frequently towards the end. The rice should be tender but hold its shape and have a barely discernible bite. Stir in the remainder of the butter and the freshly grated Parmesan cheese (the texture should be fluid and creamy). Taste and add more salt if necessary. *Serve immediately.*

Wine suggestion: Soave Classico from the Veneto area.

*How to Cook Polenta

Serves 6–8

Polenta can be served the moment it's ready or it can be turned into a wet dish and allowed to get cold. It can then be sliced and chargrilled, pangrilled, toasted or fried and served with all sorts of toppings. It can even be cut into thin slices and layered with a sauce just like Lasagne.

8 ozs (225 g/scant 1$\frac{1}{2}$ cups) coarse polenta flour (maize)
3 pints (1.7 L/7$\frac{1}{2}$ cups) water
1 level dessertsp. (2 American teasp.) salt

Put the water into a deep heavy-bottomed saucepan and bring to the boil, add salt, then sprinkle the polenta flour in very slowly letting it slip gradually through your fingers and whisking all the time (this should take 4–5 minutes). Bring to the boil and when it starts to erupt like a volcano turn the heat down to the absolute minimum — use a heat diffuser mat if you have one.

Cook for about 40 minutes stirring regularly* (I use a whisk at the beginning but as soon as the polenta comes to the boil I change to a flat bottomed spoon.) The polenta is cooked when it is very thick but not solid and comes away from the sides of the pot as you stir.

(*If you stir *constantly* on a slightly higher heat the cooking time can be reduced to about 20 minutes.)

*Soft or Wet Polenta

Polenta served in this way is wonderful with game birds or juicy meat stews. It can also be served with a rich tomato sauce and spicy sausages.

polenta as cooked in previous recipe (opposite)
4 ozs (110 g/1 stick) butter
3 ozs (85 g/$\frac{3}{4}$ cup) freshly grated Parmesan cheese (Parmigiano
   Reggiano is best)
sea salt and freshly ground pepper

As soon as the polenta is cooked add the butter, Parmesan cheese and freshly ground pepper. Taste and add a little more sea salt if necessary. Serve immediately.

Soft or wet polenta is also delicious served quite simply with fried sage leaves, melted butter and grated Parmesan cheese.

*Chargrilled Polenta

Make the polenta in the usual way (opposite). Pour the cooked polenta into a wet dish (I use a lasagne dish 9 x 7 x 2 inches/23 x 18 x 5 cm which is just perfect for this quantity, but you could use a swiss roll tin and cut into squares or diamonds when it is cold). Allow to get completely cold. Polenta can be stored like this, covered in the fridge, for several days. It make the most delicious snacks or you can make a sophisticated starter for a dinner party in just a few minutes.

To serve: Cut into slices $\frac{1}{2}$–$\frac{3}{4}$ inch (1–2 cm) thick and chargrill, pangrill or fry. Put it directly on to the bars of the grill on the highest heat without oil and cook until it is hot through and grill marked on each side. If the polenta is to be sautéed use a little olive oil or butter. Serve the slices of grilled polenta as an accompaniment to meat or fish dishes.

Chargrilled Polenta with Caramelised Onions and Pesto

Spread a slice of grilled polenta with warm caramelised onions (see p. 45) and top with a teaspoonful of pesto (see p. 55).

Chargrilled Polenta with Rocket and Olives or Roasted Red and Yellow Peppers

Arrange some fresh rocket (arugula) leaves on the grilled polenta, top with olive paste (see olive stuffing p. 42) and/or roasted red and yellow peppers (see p. 15).

Chargrilled Polenta with Tomato Fondue and Pesto

Spread 1 tablespoon of hot Tomato Fondue (see p. 75) on the grilled polenta and top with a teaspoonful of pesto (see p. 55).

Chargrilled Polenta with Gorgonzola, Cashel Blue or Goat's Cheese

Spread the hot grilled polenta with Gorgonzola, Cashel Blue or goat's cheese and serve immediately.

There are countless other possibilities. Just use your imagination and a little restraint.

Wine suggestion: Depending on how you are serving it, choose a white or red Italian wine.

Vegetables

*Lentils du Puy

Serves 4–6

Lentils du Puy are the aristocrats of the lentil family. These green speckled lentils which grow around Velley in the Auvergne have an appellation contrôlée and have now had a revival. They are very good with duck, salt pork or streaky bacon or just as a vegetable.

$\frac{1}{2}$ lb (225 g/generous 1 cup) lentils du Puy
1 carrot
1 onion, stuck with 2 cloves
bouquet garni
butter *or* extra virgin olive oil
lots of freshly squeezed lemon juice
a large handful of chopped fresh herbs e.g. fresh oregano, annual
    marjoram *or* parsley
sea salt and freshly ground pepper

Wash the lentils and put into a large saucepan. Fill with cold water, add the carrot, onion and bouquet garni, bring slowly to the boil, reduce heat and simmer very gently for 15–20 minutes, testing regularly. The lentils should be *al dente* but not hard. Drain, remove and discard the carrot, onion and bouquet garni. Season the lentils while warm with a good knob of butter or some extra virgin olive oil, then add lots of freshly squeezed lemon juice and some finely chopped herbs. Season with sea salt and freshly ground pepper. Serve immediately.

Note: Lentils are also good with a little finely chopped chilli added — say half a small chilli with seeds removed.

Ratatouille Niçoise
Mediterranean Vegetable Stew

Serves 8–10

Ratatouille, perhaps the most famous Mediterranean vegetable stew of all, can be a horrendously unappetising 'silage' — in fact it's quite difficult to get a really good result with the classic method unless you stand over the pot. For some time now I have been following Roger Vergé's example by cooking the aubergines and courgettes separately and adding them in at the end, with far better results.

> **1 lb (450 g) medium sized aubergines**
> **1 lb (450 g) courgettes (zucchini), not more than 6 inches (15 cm) long**
> **olive oil**
> **2 red peppers**
> **1 green pepper**
> **2 large cloves of garlic, crushed**
> **2 large onions, sliced — 12 ozs (340 g/3 cups)**
> **1 lb (450 g) very ripe tomatoes** *or* **1 x 14 oz (400 g) tin of tomatoes**
> **salt and freshly ground pepper**
> **$\frac{1}{2}$ teasp. coriander seeds, crushed**
> **1 tablesp. (1 American tablesp. + 1 teasp) chopped fresh basil** *or* **annual marjoram**

Slice the unpeeled aubergines and courgettes into scant $\frac{1}{4}$ inch (5 mm) rounds, sprinkle with a little salt and put into a colander. Leave for an hour to drain, then wash, drain and dry with kitchen paper. Heat about $\frac{3}{4}$ inch (2 cm) of olive oil in a frying pan, cook the aubergines and courgettes in a single layer until golden brown on each side and drain on a wire rack over an oven tray.

Cut the peppers in quarters, remove seeds and slice into $\frac{1}{4}$ inch (5 mm) strips at an angle.

Heat 2 tablespoons (2 American tablespoons + 2 teaspoons) olive oil in a wide casserole, add the sliced onions and crushed garlic, cover and sweat on a gentle heat for about 5 minutes. As they begin to soften add the sliced peppers, cover and simmer for 10–12 minutes. Meanwhile, peel and slice the tomatoes, add to the peppers and season with salt, pepper and sugar. Simmer without covering the pan until the vegetables are just cooked — about 6–8 minutes. Then add the aubergines and courgettes with the crushed coriander. Stir gently, add the basil or marjoram. Taste and correct seasoning.

Note: Ratatouille Niçoise can be served hot or cold.

Variations
Ratatouille with Olives
Add 4 ozs (110 g) whole black olives to the ratatouille about 5 minutes before the end of the cooking time.

Ratatouille with Poached Eggs

Heat 2 generous tablespoons of ratatouille per person, make a nest on a hot plate for each person and drop a poached egg into the centre — a perfect supper dish.

*French Beans

Serves 8

French beans are the great favourite of so many chefs that one eats them ad nauseam in restaurants — usually undercooked nowadays. However, there are many varieties and they can indeed be delicious. I've found that they need a lot of salt in the cooking water to bring up the flavour. They don't benefit from being kept in a hostess trolley, so if you need to cook them ahead try the method I suggest below. I think it works very well.

> **2 lbs (900 g) French beans**
> **1–2 ozs (30–55 g/$\frac{1}{4}$–$\frac{1}{2}$ stick) butter**
> **salt and freshly ground pepper**

Top and tail the beans. Bring 2 pints (1.1 L/5 cups) water to a rolling boil, add 2 teaspoons of salt and add the beans. Continue to boil very fast for 5–6 minutes or until just cooked (they should still retain a little bite). Drain immediately.* Melt a little butter in a saucepan, toss the beans in it, taste, season with freshly ground pepper and a little sea salt if necessary.

*Beans may be refreshed under cold water at this point and kept aside for several hours.

To reheat precooked beans: Just before serving, plunge into boiling salted water for 30 seconds to 1 minute, drain and toss in butter. Season and serve immediately.

Gratin Dauphinois

Serves 4–6

There are many wonderful French potato gratins that I love but if I were forced to choose one I think it would have to be this sinfully rich Gratin Dauphinois. This is a particularly good version of the classic recipe because it can be made ahead and reheated with great success.

2 lbs (900 g) even-sized potatoes
salt and freshly ground pepper
9 fl ozs (275 ml/generous 1 cup) milk
9 fl ozs (275 ml/generous 1 cup) double cream
small clove garlic, peeled and crushed
freshly grated nutmeg

Peel the potatoes with a potato peeler and slice them into very thin rounds ($\frac{1}{8}$ inch/3 mm thick). Do not wash them but dab them dry with a cloth. Spread them out on the worktop and season with salt and freshly ground pepper, mixing it in with your hands. Pour the milk into a saucepan, add the potatoes and bring to the boil. Cover, reduce the heat and simmer gently for 10 minutes.

Add the cream, garlic and a generous grating of nutmeg, and continue to simmer for 20 minutes, stirring occasionally so that the potatoes do not stick to the saucepan. Just as soon as the potatoes are cooked take them out with a slotted spoon and put them into one large or six small ovenproof dishes. Pour the creamy liquid over them*.

Reheat in a bain-marie in a preheated oven, 200°C/400°F/regulo 6, for 10–20 minutes or until they are bubbly and golden on top.

*Can be prepared ahead to this point.

Rustic Potatoes with Rosemary

Serves 4 approx.

Potatoes are served like this in both Italy and France. Other strongly flavoured herbs such as thyme, sage or bay could be used instead of rosemary.

2 lbs (900 g) old potatoes
3–4 tablesp. (4–5 American tablesp.) extra virgin olive oil
a few sprigs rosemary
1–2 cloves garlic, chopped (optional)
sea salt (Maldon if possible) and freshly ground pepper

non-stick frying pan, 10-inch (25.5 cm)

Wash and peel the potatoes and dry well. Cut in $\frac{3}{4}$ inch (2 cm) cubes and season with salt and freshly ground pepper. Heat 3–4 tablespoons olive oil in a non-stick pan over a high heat, add a few sprigs of rosemary and the potatoes, reduce the heat to medium and cook for about 20 minutes, tossing every now and then (but not too often or they won't get brown and crusty).

Towards the end of the cooking time, add the chopped garlic and toss with the potatoes but be very careful not to let it burn or it will ruin the whole dish — add more olive oil if necessary. Serve in a hot dish with a few sprigs of fresh rosemary sprinkled over the top.

Tomato Fondue

Serves 6 approx.

This wonderful tomato stew, literally 'melted tomatoes', is best made during the summer months when tomatoes are very ripe.

> 2 lbs (900 g) very ripe tomatoes
> 4 ozs (110 g/1 cup) sliced onions
> a clove of garlic, crushed (optional)
> 1 dessertsp. (2 American teasp.) extra virgin olive oil
> 1 tablesp. (1 American tablesp. + 1 teasp.) of any of the following,
>   chopped: thyme, parsley, mint, basil, lemon balm, marjoram
> salt, freshly ground pepper and sugar to taste

Sweat the sliced onions and garlic (if used) in oil on a gentle heat. It is vital for the success of this dish that the onions are completely soft before the tomatoes are added. Remove the hard core from the tomatoes. Put them into a deep bowl and cover them with boiling water. Count to 10 and then pour off the water immediately; peel off the skins, slice and add to the onions. Season with salt, freshly ground pepper and sugar and add a generous sprinkling of chopped herbs: mint or basil are my favourites. Cook for just 5 or 10 minutes more, or until the tomato softens. If you want a more concentrated tomato fondue, cook for longer.

Note: This may be served not only as a vegetable but also as a sauce, a filling or a topping for pizza; reduce a little more for a pizza or it may be too sloppy.

Piperonata

Serves 8–10

This Italian vegetable stew reheats perfectly and is a valuable stand-by to have in your fridge.

> **a clove of garlic**
> **1 onion**
> **2 tablesp. (2 American tablesp. + 2 teasp.) extra virgin olive oil**
> **2 red peppers**
> **2 green peppers**
> **6 large tomatoes (dark red and very ripe)**
> **salt, freshly ground pepper and sugar**
> **a few leaves of fresh basil**

Peel the garlic and make into a paste. Peel and slice the onion. Heat the olive oil in a casserole, add the garlic and cook for a few seconds; then add the sliced onion, toss in the oil and allow to soften over a gentle heat in a covered casserole while the peppers are being prepared. Halve the peppers, remove the seeds carefully, cut into quarters and then into $\frac{1}{4}$ inch (5 mm) strips across rather than lengthways. Add to the onion and toss in the oil; replace the lid and continue to cook.

Meanwhile peel the tomatoes (scald in boiling water for 10 seconds, pour off the water and peel immediately). Slice the tomatoes and add to the casserole, season with salt, freshly ground pepper, sugar and a few torn leaves of fresh basil if available. Cook until the vegetables are just soft — 30 minutes approx. Serve with bacon, ham, beef, monkfish, lamb etc., as a filling for omelettes, a topping for pizza or a sauce for pasta. Piperonata will keep in the fridge for 4–5 days.

Aubergines in Olive Oil

Aubergines are much loved in Italy and France, particularly in the south. Their slightly smoky flavour is very much an acquired taste, but persevere and you'll find them really delicious. Once you get hooked there are numerous recipes you can try.

For most recipes start by cutting the aubergines into $\frac{1}{2}$ inch (1 cm) thick slices, either lengthwise or in rounds. Then sprinkle them lightly with salt, stand them upright in a colander and allow to drain for about 1 hour.

To cook: Wash and dry the aubergine slices well. Heat about $\frac{3}{4}$ inch (2 cm) olive oil in a frying pan until it is hot but not smoking. Fry a few slices at a time until golden on both sides. Drain on a wire rack over a baking sheet and then serve in one of the following ways:

Aubergines with Tomato Fondue and/or Pesto
Put a spoonful of hot or cold Tomato Fondue (see p. 75) on each piece of aubergine and serve immediately, or if you wish top each one with a small blob of pesto (see p. 55).

Aubergines with Tomato and Mozzarella
Put a spoonful of Tomato Fondue (see p. 75) on each piece of fried aubergine, top it with a slice of mozzarella and sprinkle with a little freshly grated Parmesan cheese. Bake in a hot oven for 5 minutes or pop under the grill until the cheese becomes bubbly and golden.

Variation
Put a little pesto (see p. 55) on top of the Tomato Fondue and proceed as above.

Julia's Aubergines
Put a dollop of sheep's milk yoghurt on each of the slices of aubergine as soon as they are cooked, sprinkle lightly with cayenne pepper and serve warm or cold.

Melanzane di Parmigiana
Cover the base of an ovenproof dish with slices of fried aubergine, cover with a layer of Tomato Sauce (see p. 19) and sprinkle with mozzarella cheese. Continue with layers of aubergine, tomato and mozzarella until you reach the top of the dish. Finish with a layer of aubergines, sprinkle with Parmesan cheese and bake in a moderate oven for about 30 minutes until bubbly and golden on top.

Fennel with Parmesan Cheese

Serves 6

From late autumn to early spring the markets in Italy have wonderful fat fennel bulbs on offer. This crisp vegetable with its mild aniseed flavour can be eaten raw or cooked. It makes a particularly good salad thinly sliced, tossed in extra virgin olive oil and sprinkled with sea salt with perhaps a few rings of red onion or sweet red pepper mixed through.

4 large fat fennel bulbs
2 ozs (50 g/$\frac{1}{2}$ stick) butter
salt and freshly ground pepper
1 oz (30 g/$\frac{1}{4}$ cup) freshly grated Parmesan (Parmigiano Reggiano
   is best)

Garnish
freshly chopped fennel leaves

Trim the fennel of any wilted or bruised pieces. Cut off the stalky tops and sprigs of green fennel, saving the stalks for a vegetable or fish stock and keeping the leaves for garnish. Cut the fennel vertically into slices slightly less than $\frac{1}{2}$ inch (1 cm) thick.

Blanch and refresh the fennel, melt the butter in a wide saucepan, add the slices of fennel and toss gently in the butter. Season with salt and some freshly ground pepper, add a few tablespoons of water, cover the saucepan and cook on a gentle heat for about 30 minutes. Uncover the pan about $\frac{1}{2}$ way through and keep an eye on the fennel — it may need to be turned every now and then. When it is just cooked add in the grated cheese, taste and correct seasoning. Serve in a hot dish, sprinkled with freshly chopped fennel leaves.

Baked Fennel with Cream and Parmesan
Cook the fennel as above, but add 4 fl ozs (120 ml/$\frac{1}{2}$ cup) cream instead of the water. When the fennel is just cooked transfer to an ovenproof serving dish, sprinkle with grated cheese and pop under the grill until bubbly and golden. Serve immediately.

Courgettes (Zucchini) with Marjoram

Serves 4

This is a delicious way to cook courgettes. You can vary the herb — basil, thyme and freshly chopped parsley would also be good.

1 lb (450 g) green *or* golden courgettes (zucchini) *or* a mixture of
   both, no more than 5 inches (12.5 cm) in length
1–2 tablesp. ($1\frac{1}{2}$–$2\frac{1}{2}$ American tablesp.) extra virgin olive oil
1–2 teasp. annual marjoram
salt and freshly ground pepper

Top and tail the courgettes and cut them into scant $\frac{1}{4}$ inch (5 mm) thick slices. Heat the olive oil, toss in the courgettes and cook on a medium heat until tender — 4–5 minutes approx. Add the chopped marjoram. Season with salt and freshly ground pepper. Turn into a hot serving dish and serve immediately.

Green Salad with Goat's Cheese and Sundried Tomatoes

Serves 6

6–12 sundried tomatoes (see p. 80)
4–6 ozs (110–170 g) French *or* **Irish goat's cheese e.g. St Maur, Valençay, St Tola** *or* **Cais Cleire**

Green Salad
a mixture of green lettuces and salad leaves, e.g. oakleaf, rocket, butterhead, misticana, watercress, iceberg, golden marjoram, tiny spring onions

Dressing
2 tablesp. (2 American tablesp. + 2 teasp.) wine vinegar *or* **wine vinegar and balsamic vinegar mixed** *or* **freshly squeezed lemon juice**
6 tablesp. (8 American tablesp.) extra virgin olive oil
1 clove garlic, crushed
$\frac{1}{2}$ teasp. Moutarde de Meaux *or* **Lakeshore wholegrain and honey mustard**
salt and freshly ground pepper

Garnish
fresh basil leaves

To assemble: Whisk all the ingredients together for the dressing. Wash and dry the lettuces and salad leaves and tear into small pieces.

Just before serving: Toss the lettuce and salad leaves in just enough dressing to make the leaves glisten. Arrange in a wide serving dish, crumble some goat's cheese and scatter over the top. Cut the sundried tomatoes into quarters and scatter over the salad also. Sprinkle with fresh basil and serve.

Rocket and Cherry or Sundried Tomato Salad

Serves 6

> 4 ozs (110 g) fresh rocket leaves *or* a mixture of misticana and rocket
>   leaves
> red and yellow cherry tomatoes *or* sundried tomatoes
> salt, freshly ground pepper and sugar
> dressing as above

Proceed as above.

Sundried Tomatoes

Sundried tomatoes are all the rage now in both Italy and France. They can be bought at enormous expense preserved in olive oil but you can make your own quite easily. I find this method of drying them in the coolest oven of my 4-door Aga very successful. A fan oven works well also.

> very ripe tomatoes
> sea salt
> sugar
> olive oil

Cut the tomatoes in half cross-ways, put on to a wire rack, season with sea salt and sugar and drizzle with olive oil. Leave in the coolest part of a 4-door Aga, or in a fan oven at the minimum temperature, until they are totally dried out and wizened. I leave them in for 12–24 hours depending on size (after about 8 hours turn them upside down). Store in sterilised jars covered with olive oil. A few basil leaves or a couple of sprigs of rosemary, thyme or annual marjoram added to the oil make them especially delicious. Cover and keep in a cool, dry, preferably dark place. Use on salads, with pasta etc.

Desserts

Tarte Tatin

Serves 6–8

The Tatin sisters ran a restaurant at Lamotte-Beuvron in Sologne at the beginning of the century. They created this tart, some say accidentally, but however it came about it is a triumph — soft, buttery caramelised apples (or indeed you can also use pears) with crusty golden pastry underneath. It is unquestionably my favourite French tart!

$2\frac{3}{4}$ lbs (1.24 kg) approx. Golden Delicious, Cox's Orange Pippin *or* Bramley cooking apples

6 ozs (170 g) puff pastry *or* rich shortcrust pastry (see p. 23)

4 ozs (110 g/1 stick) unsalted butter

8 ozs (225 g/1 generous cup) castor sugar

heavy 8-inch (20.5 cm) copper or stainless steel saucepan with low sides

Preheat the oven to 250°C/475°F/regulo 9.

Peel, halve and core the apples. Melt the butter in the saucepan, add the sugar and cook over a medium heat until it turns slightly golden. Put the apple halves in upright, packing them in very tightly side by side. Replace the pan on a low heat and cook until the sugar and juice are a light caramel colour. Put into a hot oven for approx. 15 minutes.

Meanwhile, roll out the pastry into a round slightly larger than the saucepan. Prick it all over with a fork. Cover the apples with the pastry and nick in the edges. Put the saucepan into the fully preheated oven until the pastry is cooked and the apples are soft — 25–30 minutes approx.

Take out of the oven and rest for 5–10 minutes or longer if you like. Put a plate over the top of the saucepan and flip the tart on to a serving plate. (Watch out — this is a rather tricky operation because the hot caramel and juice can ooze out!) Reshape the tart if necessary and serve warm with softly whipped cream.

Wine suggestion: A glass of chilled dessert wine, e.g. Sauternes or Barsac. Château Coutet would be an absolute treat.

*Normandy Pear or Apple Tart

Serves 8–10

This is certainly one of the most impressive of the French tarts. It is wonderful served warm but is also very good cold, and it keeps for several days. Splash in a little kirsch if you are using pears and calvados if you are using dessert apples.

4–5 ripe pears *or* apples, poached (see p. 84)

Shortcrust pastry
7 ozs (200 g/scant 1½ cups) flour
4 ozs (110 g/1 stick) cold butter
1 egg yolk, preferably free range
pinch of salt
3–4 tablesp. (4–5 American tablesp.) cold water

Frangipane
3½ ozs (100 g/scant 1 stick) butter
3½ ozs (100 g/½ cup) castor sugar
1 egg, beaten
1 egg yolk, preferably free range
2 tablesp. (2 American tablesp. + 2 teasp.) kirsch if using pears *or* calvados if using apples
4 ozs (110 g) whole blanched almonds, ground *or* ½ ground almonds and ½ blanched and ground
1 oz (30 g/2 American tablesp.) flour

To finish
¼ pint (150 ml/generous ½ cup) approx. apricot glaze (see p. 83)
9 inch (23 cm) diameter flan ring *or* tart tin with a removable base

First make the shortcrust pastry. Sieve the flour and salt into a bowl, cut the butter into cubes and rub into the flour with the fingertips. Keep everything as cool as possible; if the fat is allowed to melt the finished pastry may be tough. When the mixture looks like coarse breadcrumbs, stop. Whisk the egg yolk and add the water.

Take a fork or knife (whichever you feel most comfortable with) and add just enough liquid to bring the pastry together, then discard the fork and collect the pastry into a ball with your hands. This way you can judge more accurately if you need a few more drops of liquid. Although slightly damp pastry is easier to handle and roll out, the resulting crust can be tough and may well shrink out of shape as the

(Clockwise from top) Normandy Pear Tart; Fruit Tartlets;Plum Tartlet; Plum Tart; Peach, Raspberry, Kiwi and Blueberry Tartlet; Pine Kernel Tart; **(centre)** Selection of Tartlets

(From left) Peaches in White Wine; Italian Fruit Salad; Strawberries in Balsamic Vinegar

(Above) Zabaglione; **(below)** Tira Misu

Nuns' Sighs

water evaporates in the oven. The drier and more difficult-to-handle pastry will give a crisper, 'shorter' crust.

Cover the pastry with cling film and leave to rest in the fridge for a minimum of 15 minutes, or better still 30 minutes. This will make the pastry much less elastic and easier to roll.

Next poach the pears (see p. 84) and allow to get cold. Preheat the oven to 180°C/350°F/regulo 4. Roll out the pastry, line the tart tin with it (see p. 84), prick lightly with a fork, flute the edges and chill again until firm. Bake blind (see p. 85) for 15–20 minutes.

Next make the frangipane. Cream the butter, gradually beat in the sugar and continue beating until the mixture is light and soft. Gradually add the egg and egg yolk, beating well after each addition. Stir in the ground almonds and flour and then add the kirsch or calvados. Pour the frangipane into the pastry case, spreading it evenly. Drain the pears well and when they are cold cut them crosswise into very thin slices, then lift the sliced pears intact and arrange them around the tart on the frangipane, pointed ends towards the centre. Arrange a final half pear in the centre.

Turn the oven up to 200°C/400°F/regulo 6. Bake the tart for 10–15 minutes until the pastry is beginning to brown. Turn down the oven heat to moderate, 180°C/350°F/regulo 4, and continue cooking for 15–20 minutes or until the fruit is tender and the frangipane is set in the centre and nicely golden.

Meanwhile make the apricot glaze (see below). When the tart is fully cooked, paint generously with apricot glaze, remove from the tin and serve warm or cold with a bowl of softly whipped cream.

Wine suggestion: A chilled dessert wine, e.g. Muscat de Beaumes de Venise.

Apricot Glaze
Apricot glaze is invaluable to have made up in your fridge. It would always be at hand in a pastry kitchen and is used to glaze tarts which contain green or orange or white fruit, e.g. kiwi, grapes, greengages, peaches, oranges, apples or pears. It will turn you into a professional at the flick of a pastry brush!

In a small saucepan (not aluminium), melt 12 ozs (350 g/1 cup) apricot jam with the juice of $\frac{1}{4}$ lemon and a very little water — just enough to make a glaze that can be poured. Push the hot jam through a nylon sieve and store in an airtight jar. Reheat the glaze to melt it before using. The quantities given above make a generous $\frac{1}{2}$ pint (300 ml/1$\frac{1}{4}$ cups) glaze.

Poached Pears

6 pears
$\frac{1}{2}$ lb (225 g/1 generous cup) sugar
1 pint (600 ml/2$\frac{1}{2}$ cups) water
a few strips of lemon peel and juice of $\frac{1}{2}$ lemon

Bring the sugar and water to the boil with the strips of lemon peel in a non-reactive saucepan. Meanwhile peel the pears thinly, cut in half and core carefully with a melon baller or a teaspoon, keeping a good shape. Put the pear halves into the syrup, cut side uppermost, add the lemon juice, cover with a paper lid and the lid of the saucepan. Bring to the boil and simmer until the pears are just soft — the tip of a knife or skewer should go through without resistance. Turn into a serving bowl, chill and serve on their own or with homemade vanilla icecream and chocolate sauce, in which case you have Poires Belle Hélène — one of Escoffier's great classics.

Pine Kernel Tart

Serves 6–8

In the Mediterranean pine kernels are gathered from under the Italian umbrella pines, *Pinis pinea*. Always buy them from a shop with a fast turnover because they tend to go rancid fairly quickly — much more so than other nuts. They do however keep very well in the freezer.

Follow the recipe for Normandy Pear Tart (see p. 82) but omit the pears/apples. Toast 2 ozs (55 g) pine kernels in a moderate oven, 180°C/350°F/regulo 4, for 8 minutes approx. or until they are pale golden. Cool and sprinkle over the frangipane before the tart goes into the oven. Brush with apricot glaze at the end of cooking and serve warm or cold.

Wine suggestion: Muscat de Beaumes de Venise.

*How to Line a Flan Ring

Use either a flan ring or a tin with a removable base. It should be at least 2 inches (5 cm) deep for a quiche.

> **Pastry made with 4 ozs (110 g) flour will line a 6–7 inch (15–18 cm) flan ring.**
> **Pastry made with 8 ozs (225 g) flour will line a 10–12 inch (25.5–30.5 cm) flan ring.**

Sprinkle the worktop and rolling pin lightly with flour and roll out the pastry quite thinly, making sure to keep it in a circular shape. The pastry should be $1\frac{1}{2}$ – 2 inches (4–5 cm) wider than the flan ring.

Sprinkle the pastry with flour, fold in half and then into quarters and then lift on to the ring. Alternatively, roll the pastry over the pin and unroll into the ring. Gently press the pastry on to the base of the tin, or if you are using a flan ring, onto the baking sheet, and right into the edges. Next press some of the overhanging pastry forward and cut off the edge by pressing it down on to the rim of the tin with your thumb. Tuck the cut edge in against the sides of the tin or flan ring and decorate the resulting rounded edge with a knife or pastry crimpers. Make sure that no pastry sticks to the outer edge or it will be difficult to remove the tin later. Prick the base of the pastry lightly with a fork.

To bake blind: Chill for 10 minutes in a fridge or 3–4 minutes in a freezer. Line the flan ring with kitchen paper and fill right to the top with dried beans or pastry weights. Bake as directed, remove the paper and beans, paint with a little beaten egg or egg white and return to the oven for 2–3 minutes. Proceed according to each recipe.

*Summer Fruit Tart

Serves 6

When I'm in France I find the selection of tarts in the pastry shop windows absolutely irresistible. In summer the market stalls are bursting with punnets of soft fruit begging to be put into rich shortcrust flans in colourful combinations.

Shortcrust pastry
4 ozs (110 g/scant 1 cup) flour
3 ozs (85 g/$\frac{3}{4}$ stick) butter
1 dessertsp. (2 American teasp.) icing sugar
pinch of salt
1 small egg, preferably free range, beaten

7 inch (18 cm) flan ring *or* tart tin with removable base

Filling
**8–12 ozs (225–340 g/2–3 cups) strawberries *or* raspberries *or*
    loganberries *or* blueberries *or* blackberries *or* a mixture**
4–6 tablesp. (5–8 American tablesp.) redcurrant jelly (see below)

Decoration
$\frac{1}{4}$ **pint (150 ml/generous $\frac{1}{2}$ cup) cream, whipped**
fresh mint *or* lemon balm leaves

Make the shortcrust pastry in the usual way (see p. 82). Line the flan ring following the instructions on p. 84 and decorate the edges. Line the pastry with kitchen paper and fill with dried beans. Bake blind in a moderate oven 180°C/350°F/regulo 4 for 20–25 minutes.

Remove paper and beans, paint the base of the tart with a little beaten egg and replace in the oven until completely cooked — 5–8 minutes. Remove and allow to cool on a wire rack.

To finish: Warm the redcurrant jelly. Paint the base of the tart with the jelly and arrange the strawberries on top, either whole or in slices. Paint the fruit so that it all looks beautifully shiny. The jelly not only glazes the fruit but also adds a delicious bitter-sweet flavour.

Decorate with tiny rosettes of cream and mint or lemon balm leaves.

Note: This tart shell can be used for many other types of fruit, e.g. kiwi fruit, peeled and pipped grapes, bananas, plums, peaches, or nectarines. Brush with apricot glaze (see p. 83) if yellow or green fruit is used.

Wine suggestion: A chilled dessert wine, e.g. Coteaux du Layon from the Loire Valley.

Redcurrant Jelly for Glaze

Makes 3 pots approx.

> **2 lbs (900 g/8 cups) redcurrants**
> **2 lbs (900 g/4$\frac{1}{2}$ cups) granulated sugar**

Remove the string from the redcurrants either by hand or with a fork. Put the redcurrants and sugar into a wide stainless steel saucepan and stir continuously until they come to the boil. Boil for exactly 8 minutes, stirring only if they appear to be sticking to the bottom. Skim carefully.

Turn into a nylon sieve and allow to drip through (do not push the pulp through or the jelly will be cloudy). You can stir it gently once or twice just to free the bottom of the sieve of pulp.

Pour the jelly into sterilised pots immediately. Redcurrants are very high in pectin so the jelly will begin to set just as soon as it begins to cool.

Note: Unlike most other fruit jellies, this one needs no water.

*Plum, Greengage or Apricot Tart

Serves 10–12

Makes 1 x 11 inch (28 cm) or 2 x 7 inch (18 cm) tarts

Pastry
8 ozs (225 g/scant 2 cups) flour
4 ozs (110 g/1 stick) butter
2 tablesp. (2 American tablesp. + 2 teasp.) icing sugar
1 large egg, preferably free range
1 tablesp. (1 American tablesp. + 1 teasp.) approx. water

Filling
18–20 plums, greengages *or* apricots depending on size
1 oz (30 g/$\frac{1}{4}$ stick) butter
3–4 tablesp. (4–5 American tablesp.) castor sugar
redcurrant jelly (opposite) *or* apricot glaze (optional — see p. 83)

Make the pastry in the usual way (see p. 82). Cover and allow to rest for 30 minutes in a refrigerator. Preheat the oven to 180°C/350°F/regulo 4. Roll out the pastry, line the tart tin or tins (see p. 84), fill with kitchen paper and dried beans and bake blind for 15–20 minutes. Remove the beans and paper.

Cut the plums in half, discard the stones and arrange cut side up on the tart, packing in quite tightly at an angle because they will shrink in cooking. Sprinkle with castor sugar and dot with butter. Cook in a moderate oven for 30–45 minutes until the fruit is really soft and slightly scorched. Serve the tart warm just as it is with some softly whipped cream or paint with redcurrant jelly or apricot glaze thinned out with some of the juices.

Wine suggestion: A chilled dessert wine, e.g. Muscat de Rivesaltes from the Midi.

Peach or Nectarine Tart

Serves 10–12

pastry as above
7–8 peaches *or* nectarines
4 tablesp. (5 American tablesp. + 1 teasp.) castor sugar
juice of $\frac{1}{2}$ lemon
1 oz (30 g/$\frac{1}{4}$ stick) butter

Cut the fruit in half and remove the stones, sprinkle with the lemon juice and castor sugar and allow to macerate while you bake the pastry blind (see p. 85). Fill the tart shell with the fruit, pour over the juice, dot with the butter and bake as above.

Wine suggestion: A chilled dessert wine, e.g. Muscat de Rivesaltes from the Midi.

*Confiture de Vieux Garçons
Old Boys' Jam!

This delicious boozy way of preserving summer fruit is great fun to do, but it only works if you use really good quality fruit — preferably unsprayed — and good quality spirit. I use vodka but others favour rum or brandy. You need a large glass or earthenware pot, preferably with a wide mouth and a lid. Glass ones are on sale readily in France, and a German Rumtopf jar is perfect.

> **2 lbs (900 g) best quality strawberries, hulled**
> **1 lb (450 g/2 generous cups) castor sugar**
> **1 bottle vodka, $1\frac{3}{4}$ pints (1 L/$4\frac{1}{2}$ cups)**
> **2 lbs (900 g/8 cups) raspberries**
> **1 lb (450 g/2 generous cups) castor sugar**
> **2 lbs (900 g/8 cups) loganberries**
> **1 lb (450 g/2 generous cups) castor sugar**
> **1 lb (450 g) peaches** *and/or* **apricots, stoned**
> **$\frac{1}{2}$ lb (225 g/1 generous cup) castor sugar**
> **1 lb (450 g) plums** *and/or* **greengages, stoned and halved**
> **$\frac{1}{2}$ lb (225 g/1 generous cup) castor sugar**

Put the strawberries into a well washed glass or earthenware pot, sprinkle with the sugar and leave overnight. Next day pour on the vodka, put a sterilised plate on top to keep down the fruit, cover the top with cling film and the lid and keep in a dark place. Add more soft fruit and sugar as they come into season. Top up with alcohol as is necessary and sterilise the plate each time (the fruit should be well covered with liquid). When the pot is just about full, add a final dose of alcohol and put away until Christmas (or at least a month!). Serve sparingly with softly whipped cream or ice cream. Any spare liquid could be diluted with champagne for a delicious aperitif.

*Strawberries in Balsamic Vinegar

Serves 6

Marcella Hazan first introduced me to this unlikely sounding combination. It takes a certain amount of courage to try it but believe me it makes strawberries taste exquisitely intense. Aceto Balsamico, the aristocrat of Italian vinegars, varies enormously; it is precious and expensive so buy the best one you can find and use it sparingly.

 2 lbs (900 g) strawberries
 3–5 tablesp. (4–6 American tablesp.) castor sugar
 1–2 tablesp. ($1\frac{1}{2}$–$2\frac{1}{2}$ American tablesp.) Balsamic vinegar
   (aceto balsamico)

About 30 minutes before serving, remove the hulls from the berries and cut in half lengthways. Sprinkle with sugar and toss gently. Just before serving add the balsamic vinegar and toss again. Serve immediately.

Note: This recipe is not successful with wine or malt vinegars.

*Peaches or Nectarines in White Wine

Serves 6–8

In Italy fresh fruit is usually served after dinner in some form or another. A favourite ritual is to slice a perfect peach into your glass of white wine, leave it to macerate for a few minutes, eat the peach slices with your fingers and then drink the wine.

 6 perfect peaches *or* nectarines
 $\frac{1}{2}$ pint (300 ml/$1\frac{1}{4}$ cups) sweet Italian Moscato *or* dry white wine
 $2\frac{1}{2}$–3 tablesp. (3–4 American tablesp.) castor sugar (the amount
   depends on how dry the wine is)

Put the peaches or nectarines into a deep bowl, pour boiling water over them, leave for 20–30 seconds, drain and drop into iced water. Pull off the peel, cut into $\frac{1}{4}$ inch (5 mm) slices and sprinkle with sugar. Pour on the white wine, chill in the refrigerator and allow to macerate for an hour.

Sugared Peaches with Fresh Lemon Juice
Another fresh-tasting version of this recipe is made with lemon juice instead of wine. Use the juice of 1–2 lemons.

Wine suggestion: Chilled Italian Moscato.

*Italian Fruit Salad

Serves 4-6

This recipe, made in seconds, makes a delicious fresh fruit salad. Use the best fruit you can find — the combination can vary. Marcella Hazan made it for me with wild berries from the woods and it was quite exquisite. She dressed it at the table just before we ate it.

> 4 ozs (110 g/1 cup) blackberries
> 4 ozs (110 g/1 cup) blueberries
> 4 ozs (110 g/1 cup) wild strawberries (fraises du bois) *or*
>   small strawberries
> 4 ozs (110 g/1 cup) raspberries
> 1 or 2 peaches *or* nectarines
> juice of $\frac{1}{2}$ – 1 lemon
> 2 ozs (55 g/scant $\frac{1}{4}$ cup) sugar
> fresh mint leaves (optional)

Combine the berries and the sliced peaches or nectarines in a bowl and sprinkle with sugar and fresh lemon juice. Tear some fresh mint leaves into the fruit, stir, taste and add more sugar or juice if necessary. Serve immediately.

Wine suggestion: A chilled sparkling Italian wine, e.g. Asti Spumante from Piedmont.

*Zabaglione

Serves 4

This is possibly everyone's favourite Italian dessert. Marsala is best in it but you can use a mixture of dark rum and sweet sherry instead.

> 4 egg yolks, preferably free range
> 4 tablesp. (5 American tablesp. + 1 teasp.) castor sugar
> 8 tablesp. (10 American tablesp. + 2 teasp.) Marsala
> 8–12 sponge fingers

> 1 bowl, 4 pint (2.3 L/10 cups) capacity

Bring a saucepan of water to the boil. Separate the eggs, put the yolks into the bowl with the castor sugar and whisk for a few seconds until they fluff up. Sit the bowl into a saucepan of simmering water, add the Marsala whisking all the time and continue until the zabaglione is light and fluffy and has increased enormously in volume—about 5–8 minutes with an electric whisk or 15 minutes by hand. Pour immediately into warm glasses, put each one on a plate and serve at once with a few sponge fingers to dunk in the boozy fluff.

Zabaglione is also delicious served with fresh summer berries.

Wine suggestion: A glass of Marsala.

Honey and Lavender Ice-cream

Serves 8–10

This ice-cream reminds me of the lavender fields of Provence humming with bees collecting nectar for lavender honey. The heavy scent permeates the air for miles — pure magic!

6 fl ozs (175 ml/$\frac{3}{4}$ cup) Provençal lavender honey *or* pure Irish honey
40 sprigs of fresh lavender *or* less of dried (use the blossom end only)
8 fl ozs (250 ml/1 cup) milk
16 fl ozs (475 ml/2 cups) cream
6 egg yolks, preferably free range

Garnish
sprigs of lavender

Put the milk and cream into a heavy-bottomed saucepan with the lavender sprigs, bring to the boil and leave to infuse for 15–20 minutes. Whisk the egg yolks, add a little of the lavender-flavoured liquid and then mix the two together. Cook over a low heat until the mixture barely thickens and lightly coats the back of a spoon. Melt the honey gently, just to liquify, and add to the custard. Chill thoroughly and freeze, preferably in an ice-cream maker.

Serve garnished with sprigs of lavender.

Wine suggestion: A chilled dessert wine, e.g. a Vendange Tardive from Alsace.

*Tira Misu

Serves 8

The name means pick-me-up, and not surprising either, considering the amount of booze! This is a fairly recent Italian pudding which seems to have originated in Venice but which is now served in restaurants all over Italy, and it always tastes different. We've had rave reviews for this version which is very easily put together. Mascarpone cheese, which is an essential ingredient, is now becoming more widely available.

> 38–40 boudoir biscuits
> 8 fl oz (250 ml/1 cup) strong espresso coffee (if your freshly made
>   coffee is not strong enough, add 1 teasp. instant coffee)
> 4 tablesp. (5 American tablesp. + 1 teasp.) brandy
> 2 tablesp. (2 American tablesp. + 2 teasp.) Jamaica rum
> 3 ozs (85 g) dark chocolate
> 3 eggs, separated — preferably free range
> 4 tablesp. (5 American tablesp. + 1 teasp.) castor sugar
> 9 ozs (255 g/generous 1 cup) Mascarpone cheese*
>
> dish 10 x 8 inches (20.5–25.5 cm) with low sides

Mix the coffee with the brandy and rum. Roughly grate the chocolate (we do it in the food processor with the pulse button). Whisk the egg yolks with the sugar until it reaches the 'ribbon' stage and is light and fluffy, then fold in the Mascarpone a tablespoon at a time.

Whisk the egg whites stiffly and fold gently into the cheese mixture. Now you are ready to assemble the Tira Misu.

Dip each side of the boudoir biscuits one at a time into the coffee mixture and arrange side by side in the dish. Spread half the Mascarpone mixture gently over the biscuits, sprinkle half the grated chocolate over the top, then another layer of soaked biscuits and finally the rest of the Mascarpone. Cover the whole bowl carefully with cling film or better still slide it into a plastic bag and twist the end. Refrigerate for at least 6 hours — I usually make it the day before I use it.

Just before serving scatter the remainder of the chocolate over the top and serve. Some recipes use unsweetened cocoa here, but I love very good quality bitter dark chocolate.

Note: Tira misu will keep for several days in a fridge but make sure it is covered so that it doesn't pick up 'fridgie' tastes.

*Mascarpone, a delicious rich creamy cheese which originated in Lodi in Lombardy, is made by curdling cream with citric acid. It is often used instead of cream with fruit and pastries. If you have difficulty locating it contact Horgan's Delicatessen, Mitchelstown, Co. Cork, tel. (025) 24977 for your nearest supplier.

Wine suggestion: A glass of chilled rich, raisiny Italian dessert wine, e.g. Vin Santo.

Sospiri di Monaca
Nuns' Sighs

Makes 40

These delicious little hazelnut meringues are made all over Sicily. The myth of nuns being trapped inside the convent walls fantasising about what they may be missing is popular in many parts of Italy and lots of confections are made, supposedly to cheer up the good sisters!

> 7 ozs (200 g/scant $1\frac{1}{2}$ cups) hazelnuts
> 4 egg whites, preferably free range
> 10 ozs (285 g/$2\frac{1}{2}$ cups) icing sugar
> finely grated zest of 1 lemon

Preheat the oven to 180°C/350°F/regulo 4.

Spread the hazelnuts out on a baking tray and put into the preheated oven for 15 minutes approx. or until the skins loosen. Rub off the skins in a tea towel and chop the nuts as finely as possible.

Put the egg whites and the sieved icing sugar into a spotlessly clean bowl and whisk until the mixture reaches stiff peaks. Gently fold in the chopped hazelnuts and lemon zest. Spoon out the meringue in generous blobs with a teaspoon on to baking sheets lined with silicone paper or oiled tin foil. Tease the little blobs into tear shapes. Bake at 150°C/300°F/regulo 2 for 45 minutes. Allow to cool.

Serve with a cup of coffee. They are also wonderful with a few raspberries or a perfect peach and a blob of cream.

Note: Like all meringues, Nuns' Sighs will keep for ages in an airtight tin.

Breads

I still get a buzz every time I take a loaf of crusty bread out of the oven. For years and years I have loved making bread, so I'm delighted to see that there is now a very real breadmaking revival. Homemade bread is high fashion — food critics lavish praise on the restaurants that bake their own, and it has now become quite a status symbol.

Apart from that, more and more professional people are discovering how therapeutic it is to come home, toss the briefcase aside and start kneading (men particularly!). Now that the peasant breads of Italy and France are all the rage, there are more things to try than ever before. All you need is imagination and away you go.

Brioche

Makes 15–20 individual brioches *or* 2 large ones

Brioche is the richest of all yeast doughs and absolutely irresistible to eat. Some recipes can be intimidating but this very easy version works well and I've designed it so that the dough can rise overnight in the fridge and be shaped and baked in the morning. In France, brioche is traditionally baked in fluted tins but it can of course be baked in any size or shape, either free form or moulded. The individual *brioches à tête*, which literally means brioches with a head, are usually eaten warm for breakfast with butter and homemade jam. The dough can also be used for all sort of 'grand' recipes — anything from Saucisson en Brioche to a whole fish encased in brioche dough — Saumon or Loup de Mer en Croûte, for example. Pretty impressive!

$\frac{1}{2}$ oz (15 g) fresh yeast (*or* use half quantity of dried yeast)
2 ozs (55 g/generous $\frac{1}{4}$ cup) castor sugar
2$\frac{1}{2}$ fl ozs (63 ml/generous $\frac{1}{4}$ cup) tepid water
4 eggs, preferably free range
1 lb (450 g/3 generous cups) strong white flour
large pinch of salt
8 ozs (225 g/2 sticks) soft unsalted butter

egg wash made with 1–2 beaten eggs, preferably free range

15–20 individual moulds *or* 2 large moulds

Dissolve the yeast and sugar in the water, add the beaten eggs and pour into a mixing bowl. Add the flour and salt and mix to a stiff dough either by hand or with the dough hook of an electric mixer. When the mixture is smooth, beat in the butter in small pieces. The finished dough should have a silky appearance. Place it in an oiled bowl, cover and rest it overnight in the fridge.

Next day, knead the dough lightly, weigh into 2 oz (55 g) pieces and roll it into balls. With the side of your hand make a deep indent into each ball of dough slightly off centre. Put the dough (heavy end first) into well buttered brioche moulds. Push the 'little hat' towards the centre, leaving it just protruding above the body of the dough.* Brush the top of each brioche with egg wash.

Allow them to prove in a warm place until they have doubled in size. Preheat the oven to 180°C/350°F/regulo 4. Egg wash the brioches again. Cook for 20–25 minutes. Serve freshly baked with butter and home-made strawberry jam.

Large brioches will take 40–50 minutes approx. to cook. A skewer insert-ed into the centre should come out clean.

*They can be frozen at this stage.

Cheese Brioche

Makes 1 loaf

This is really scrummy, particularly when eaten warm.

> $\frac{1}{2}$ **quantity brioche dough (opposite)**
> $3\frac{1}{2}$ **–4 ozs (100–110 g/$\frac{1}{2}$ cup) coarsely grated Gruyère cheese**
> **egg wash as in previous recipe**

1 loaf tin, 9 inch (23 cm) x 5 inch (12.5 cm) x 2 inch (5 cm)

Preheat the oven to 200°C/400°F/regulo 6.

Knead $\frac{3}{4}$ of the cheese into the dough after it has been knocked back (see p. 44), put into a well buttered loaf tin and brush with egg wash. Allow to double in size, egg wash again, sprinkle with the remainder of the cheese and bake for 15 minutes, then reduce the temperature to moderate, 180°C/350°F/regulo 4, for 25–30 minutes approx. Remove from the tin and cool on a wire rack.

*Focaccia
Italian Flat Bread

Makes 4

Serves 16 approx.

Foccaccia is a flat bread which was introduced to Sicily by the Greeks. Schiacciata, as it is called in Tuscany, can now be found all over Italy and appears in many smart restaurants from Naples to New York. When you taste it you'll understand why it's salty tang becomes addictive, and there are many variations on the theme.

> $1\frac{1}{2}$ lbs (690 g/$5\frac{1}{4}$ cups) white yeast bread dough (see p. 43)
> olive oil and sea salt

Divide the dough into 4 pieces and roll out each piece to about $\frac{1}{2}$ inch (1 cm) thickness. Put on to an oiled baking sheet and make indentations all over the surface with your fingers. Brush the surface liberally with olive oil and sprinkle with sea salt.

Allow the focaccia to rise again. Preheat the oven to 230°C/450°F/regulo 8, bake for 5 minutes and then reduce temperature to 200°C/400°F/regulo 6 and bake for a further 10 minutes.

Variations

Focaccia with Rosemary
Another favourite is to sprinkle 2 teaspoons of finely chopped rosemary over the oil and then sprinkle with sea salt and proceed as above.

Focaccia with Sage
Knead 2 teaspoons of finely chopped sage into the piece of dough, then roll out to $\frac{1}{2}$ inch (1 cm) thickness, and brush with olive oil. Make indentations all over the surface with your fingertips, sprinkle with sea salt, then proceed as above.

Focaccia with Black Olives
Substitute 1–2 tablespoons of stoned black olives for the sage and proceed as above. 1 teaspoon of chopped marjoram or thyme leaves is a delicious addition here also.

*Bruschetta
Garlic and Olive Oil Bread

Serves 4

This toasted or chargrilled bread rubbed with garlic and drizzled with olive oil is found right down through Italy from Tuscany to Apulia. It was once the traditional lunch of shepherds and peasants and has now become a fashionable appetiser. That's not surprising, because made with really good bread and extra virgin olive oil it becomes addictive. In Tuscany it is called Fett'unta meaning 'oiled slice', and in the south very ripe tomato is also rubbed into the chargrilled bread.

> 4 slices of crusty country white bread, $\frac{3}{4}$ inch (2 cm) thick
> 1 clove garlic
> extra virgin olive oil

Toast or chargrill the bread on both sides and rub immediately with a cut clove of garlic. Drizzle with olive oil and serve.

Variations
Bruschetta with Rocket and Black Olive Paste
Arrange a few rocket leaves on a slice of bruschetta, top with a spoonful of tapenade or olive paste (see p. 42) and serve immediately.

Bruschetta with Tomatoes and Marjoram or Basil
Chop one or two very ripe tomatoes into rough dice, mix with a little freshly chopped marjoram or basil, season with salt, freshly ground pepper and sugar and spread on the warm bruschetta. Serve immediately.

Bruschetta with Rocket and Roasted Peppers
Arrange a few rocket leaves on a slice of bruschetta, top with squares of roasted red and yellow peppers, drizzle with extra virgin olive oil and a few fresh basil leaves.

Bruschetta with Rocket and Shavings of Parmesan
Arrange a few fresh rocket leaves on a slice of warm bruschetta, put a few shavings of Parmesan on top (Parmigiano Reggiano is best), drizzle with extra virgin olive oil and serve immediately.

A selection of three of these served on a plate would make a delicious starter.

Wine suggestion: Chilled white Orvieto from Umbria or a young Chianti.